Radical Collections

Re-examining the roots of collections, practices
and information professions

Radical Collections

Re-examining the roots of collections, practices and information professions

Edited by Jordan Landes and Richard Espley

SENATE HOUSE LIBRARY
UNIVERSITY OF LONDON

Senate House Library
University of London
Senate House
Malet Street, London WC1E 7HU

www.senatehouselibrary.ac.uk

2018

This book is also available online at http://humanities-digital-library.org.

ISBN 978-1-913002-00-8 (paperback edition)
ISBN 978-1-913002-01-5 (PDF edition)
ISBN 978-1-913002-03-9 (ePub edition)
ISBN 978-1-913002-02-2 (.mobi edition)

Contents

Notes on contributors

Julio Cazzasa is special collections cataloguer for Senate House Library, University of London.

Since completing his doctorate on Djuna Barnes, **Richard Espley** has published on Barnes and other modernists, the literary portrayal of London Zoo, commemorative representations of the First World War and issues of censorship in the modernist period. He has worked professionally in libraries for some years and is currently head of modern collections at Senate House Library, University of London.

Kirsty Fife is an archivist and academic based in Leeds, Yorkshire. She is currently about to start PhD research at UCL, exploring methods for documenting and archiving UK-based DIY music subcultures. Prior to this she worked as an archivist for organisations including the National Science and Media Museum, Parliamentary Archives and Hoxton Hall.

Hannah Henthorn will qualify as an archivist in 2019 after completing her studies with the University of Dundee, for which she was awarded the National Archives Diversity Education Bursary. Based in Edinburgh, she has been working as a local studies and archives assistant, in North Lanarkshire, since July 2018, and has previously worked for the National Records of Scotland and Aberdeen Art Gallery. She has also volunteered at several archives and heritage organisations. Her research interests include early modern political history, the representation of marginalised groups in finding aids and catalogues, and youth engagement with archives.

Jordan Landes was research librarian for history at Senate House Library. She is the author of *London Quakers in the trans-atlantic world: the creation of an early modern community* (Palgrave, 2015) and continues her research in Quaker history.

Mairéad Mooney is a PhD Excellence Scholar in the School of English, University College Cork. She is researching children's literature and libraries in Ireland in the early decades of the post-independence period.

Katherine Quinn is a PhD researcher in the University of Warwick's sociology department. Her ethnography of the integrated library The Hive in Worcester explores concepts of classification, boundaries and belonging through an affective lens, and will be submitted in 2019.

Lucas Richert is a chancellor's fellow in history, University of Strathclyde and the incoming George Urdang Chair in the History of Pharmacy, University of Wisconsin-Madison. Richert is the author of *Conservatism, Consumer Choice and the Food and Drug Administration during the Reagan Era: A Prescription for Scandal* (Lexington Books, 2014), which won the Arthur Miller Centre First Book Prize in 2015, and the forthcoming *Strange Trips: Science, Culture, and the Regulation of Drugs* (McGill-Queen's University Press, 2019).

Alycia Sellie is the associate librarian for collections at the Graduate Center Library, part of the City University of New York. Her work has appeared in works such as *Libraries and the Reading Public in Twentieth Century America, Feminist Collections*, and her own publication, *The Borough is My Library: A Metropolitan Library Workers Zine*.

Introduction: Radical collections and radical voices

Jordan Landes

'Radical' is defined in the *Oxford English Dictionary* as the advocation of 'thorough and far-reaching political or social reform … characterized by independence of or departure from what is usual or traditional'. Senate House Library's (SHL) 'Radical Voices' season, which took place in the first half of 2017, reached beyond late eighteenth- and early nineteenth-century use of the word to describe the Liberal Party's stance on reform. Moreover, the programme, which included an exhibition of items from SHL collections and a series of events, embraced the word to represent the hard work of those who more generally advocated for societal improvements.[1]

One of the highlights was a conference entitled 'Radical Collections: Radicalism and Libraries and Archives'. Its call for papers asked potential speakers to consider four questions that can be simplified into who, what, how and what now? More specifically, the conference organisers sought papers considering *who* works in libraries and archives and *who* uses them? Next we asked *what* is in collections and how are collections being developed? Once books, manuscripts and resources are brought together, *how* are they organised? Furthermore, what is the impact of information professionals' decisions? Lastly, *what is happening now* and what current events are being held in libraries, archives and the information professions? The call for papers was clear that it welcomed proposals encompassing diverse periods, locations and topics.

As stated in the call for papers, as centres of published and unpublished information, libraries and archives have an impact on the dissemination of knowledge. There are consequences for materials, users and the perception of the field as a result of who enters the information professions. These issues are all set within the current decisions regarding funding, closures and technological change. Priorities for accepting and accessioning collections have been and are based on a variety of reasons. For example, since it was established in 1922, the Trades Union Congress (TUC) Library Collections, London Metropolitan University, has gathered together, preserved and made

---

1 'Radical, adj. and n.', OED Online, (Oxford University Press). See http://0-www.oed.com. catalogue.libraries.london.ac.uk/view/Entry/157251?rskey=4iWRyc&result=1&isAdvanced =false (accessed 18 Apr. 2018).

available materials related to trade unions and collective bargaining, and has maintained this specialisation.[2] The Bishopsgate Library serves as part of the Bishopsgate Institute's vision; that is, it is 'dedicated to opening minds, challenging perceptions and enriching lives'. As such, the library's strengths have developed intentionally and through donation into key collections on London and the labour, co-operative, freethought and humanist movement, including feminist and women's history; lesbian gay bisexual transgender and queer history; and protest and campaigning.[3] More recently, the Black Cultural Archives was established in 1981 as the national repository 'dedicated to collecting, preserving and celebrating the histories of diverse people of African and Caribbean descent in Britain'. Their collections began as a community archive and 'constitute a permanent record of the richness of the Black experience in Britain and … [are] accessible to all'.[4]

Work in the past decades, and especially the last one, by archives and archivists prompts all of us in the information professions to rethink our collections and the very act of collecting. Historian Howard Zinn wrote about archives in 1977, pointing out that the collections tended to be biased toward 'the important and powerful people of the society', to focus on the individual over movements, and to emphasise the 'past over the present'.[5] He challenged archivists to 'compile a whole new world of documentary material, about the lives, desires, needs, of ordinary people'.[6] Change, whether legal, societal, technological or any other driver, requires us to ask questions about the present reality of information services and collections and to keep asking questions throughout our careers in order to keep moving towards the type of collections envisaged by Zinn and others. 'Documenting the Now' (DocNow) and its 'strong commitment to prioritizing ethical practices when working with social media content, especially in terms of collection and long-term preservation', is a recent example of a project devoted to such work, particularly in this new format.[7] Archivist Jarrett M. Drake wrote in April 2017 that American 'libraries should be on the frontlines to fight fascism because

2   Archives Hub, 'TUC Library Collections, London Metropolitan University'. See https://archiveshub.jisc.ac.uk/search/locations/8ee6b2c9-81a8-3854-b684-c81484f66384 (accessed 18 Apr. 2018).

3   'Bishopsgate Institute: About Us', at www.bishopsgate.org.uk/content.aspx?CategoryID=964&ArticleID=1548&fp=1; and 'Bishopsgate Institute: Special Collections and Archives' at www.bishopsgate.org.uk/Library/Special-Collections-and-Archives (both accessed 18 Apr. 2018).

4   'About the Black Cultural Archives' at https://blackculturalarchives.org/about/; and 'Black Cultural Archives: Collections' at https://blackculturalarchives.org/collections/ (both accessed 18 Apr. 2018)

5   Howard Zinn, 'Secrecy, archives, and the public interest', *Midwestern Archivist*, 2 (2) (1977): 14–27 at 21–2. See http://digital.library.wisc.edu/1793/44118 (accessed 9 Apr. 2018); Jarret M. Drake, 'I'm leaving the archive profession: it's better this way', *On Archivy* (occasional writing about the archive), 24 Apr. 2017, https://medium.com/on-archivy/im-leaving-the-archival-profession-it-s-better-this-way-ed631c6d72fe (accessed 18 Apr. 2018).

6   Zinn, 'Secrecy, archives,and the public interest', p. 25.

7   See 'About', DocNow, www.docnow.io/ (accessed 18 Apr. 2018).

the control of information and ideas is central to the spread of fascism, and thus libraries will be forced either to endorse that spread or encumber it.[8] As information professionals, we have opportunities to examine and re-examine collections in our care and those that can or should be in our care. We can call them 'radical collections', although perhaps we should just call them 'collections', and we can choose to continue to work towards the goal of collecting broadly and fairly. Indeed, Chris Bourg and nina de jesus, among many others, remind us that libraries are not neutral, as institutions that 'were created not only for a specific ideological purpose but for an ideology that is fundamentally oppressive in nature'.[9]

Our reasons for hosting the Radical Voices season at SHL, and particularly the Radical Collections conference emerged from the collections that the library has developed over the years since it was founded. Like the libraries mentioned above, SHL's history is another example of how libraries and archives have either actively or even passively gathered together books, manuscripts and ephemera produced by groups or individuals advocating change. The library's origins lie in the two hundred books that were part of the provision when the University of London was founded, then subsequent purchases in 1839 and 1846 and large donations in the 1870s. Among those donations was that of George Grote, classical historian and Vice Chancellor of the University from 1862 to 1871. His collection came to the library after his death. Before he was involved in politics, and continuing through his time as a Member of Parliament, Grote argued for democratic reform and universal suffrage.[10] While his collection included the books of his chosen discipline, a large number of the books reflected his radical beliefs, with works exploring the expansion of democracy and popular power, including quite a few on the French Revolution.

The SHL's role as a home for collections that have evolved from radical beliefs continued into the twentieth century, with volumes absorbed from the London Institution, an organisation that provided lectures, reading rooms and a library to subscribers including Dissenters, and allowed women to attend lectures.[11] Even now, the library's acquisition goals remain the same as they

---

8   Jarrett M. Drake, 'How libraries can trump the trend to make America hate again', a panel talk given at the 2017 meeting of the British Columbia Library Association, published at On Archivy, 24 Apr. 2017. See https://medium.com/on-archivy/how-libraries-can-trump-the-trend-to-make-america-hate-again-8a4170df1906 (accessed 18 Apr. 2018).

9   Chris Bourg 'Never neutral: Libraries, technology, and inclusion', published at Feral Librarian, 2015, January 28. See https://chrisbourg.wordpress.com/2015/01/28/never-neutral-libraries-technology-and-inclusion/ (accessed 9 Aug. 2018) and nina de jesus, 'Locating the Library in Institutional Oppression', In the Library with the Lead Pipe, 24 September 2014. See www.inthelibrarywiththeleadpipe.org/2014/locating-the-library-in-institutional-oppression/ (accessed 8 Aug. 2018).

10   See J. Hamburger, 23 Sep. 2004, Grote, George (1794–1871), historian and politician, Oxford Dictionary of National Biography at www.oxforddnb.com.catalogue.libraries.london.ac.uk/ (accessed 14 Mar. 2018).

11   K.E. Attar, 'Incunabula at Senate House Library: growth of a collection', Library and Information History, 25 (2) (Jun. 2009): 97–116 at 100–1; and London Institution, A Catalogue of the Library

were more than a century ago. The Ron Heisler collection, described at length in Julio Cazzasa's contribution, is a newer chapter in the SHL biography, and the current archivists and librarians maintain the tradition. This description is the story of one university library, however each library and archive has its own particular origins and has built upon them. Sharing their experiences of the collections in their institutions allows information professionals to take the opportunity to learn, empathise and develop connections, a fact which inspired one particular event during SHL's Radical Voices season.

On 3 March, more than a hundred people came together at Radical Collections to hear twelve talks; and for nine hours, librarians, archivists, students, historians and other interested attendees spoke, listened, discussed and tweeted about issues ranging from, in the words of the conference's call for papers, 'selection, accession and collection development' to 'cataloguing, classification and arrangement, activities that librarians and archivists are in positions to widen or limit access to materials through various means'. Librarians and archivists from across the sector, from national and public libraries, universities and special libraries, congregated with trainee librarians and archivists, and other interested historians and social scientists in the Institute of Historical Research's Wolfson Suite.

A conscious organisational decision was made to include papers about libraries *and* archives, focusing on collecting and collections rather than types. Convergence of libraries, archives and museums (so-called LAMs) has been addressed in the past two decades, and this conference mostly served to highlight what the different repositories had in common. In the absence of similar standards of description and different cataloguing, some discussion required sympathy rather than empathy among the different professionals, but the preservation and organisation of information remained the shared thread. In essence, this conference was based on David Gracy's description of LAMs as 'fields uniting in the information domain and joined in the stewardship of the cultural record'. For Gracy, '[u]nifying all these fields of the Information domain are the collections of recorded knowledge – their creation, organization, preservation, and utilization – that form the cultural record'.[12] And as Deanna Marcum wrote in 2014, attendees of this conference saw 'well beyond the confines of functional divides'.[13]

As a collection of papers from a conference, this volume represents research and topics that were discussed on a single day and cannot address the many concerns and changes related to current collecting and

---

of the London Institution Systematically Classed: an historical and bibliographical account of the establishment. Volume I: The General Library (London: C. Skipper and East, 1835), p. vi.

12   David B. Gracy II, 'Welcome to the premier issue', *Libraries & the Cultural Record*, 41 (3) (2006): 295, at http://muse.jhu.edu/journals/libraries_and_culture/v041/41.3gracy.html (accessed 11 Jul. 2018).

13   Deanna Marcum, 'Archives, libraries, museums: coming back together?', *Information & Culture*, 49 (1) (Austin, TX: University of Texas Press, 2014): 74–89 at 86. See www.utexaspressjournals. org/doi/abs/10.7560/IC49105 (accessed 11 Jul. 2018).

collections. Gina Schlesselman-Tarango asked how librarians can critique the organisations in which we work with their vestigial power structures, citing Todd Honma's question, 'how do we challenge the weight of history that continues to haunt our everyday practices?'.[14] While a number of papers presented at the conference addressed various aspects of intersectionality, it can be noted that all of the speakers at the conference were white, as are the authors of the chapters included in this volume, and its editors. 'Librarianship has long been one of the whitest professions, and the demographics of librarianship have hardly shifted over the last generation',[15] and the wider information professions are little different. But to quote Honma again, 'critical self-reflection about LIS and our role in it is crucial to make our field more just, equitable, and accessible for all, rather than just a privileged few'.[16]

Two of its panel sessions focused on archival and library collections, discussing the act of amassing artefacts and the associated challenges, management of these collections and aspects of items within them. The question of collecting radically begins early in the process, such as Siobhan Britton's point that zines are acquired through traditional finance systems or Amy Todman's account of the difficulties of collecting from 'radical' organisations, an example being the National Library of Scotland's work on the archives from Engender, Scotland's membership feminist organisation. Two talks looked at how such collections can be employed, with that of Lisa Redlinski and John Wrighton encompassing classroom use of progressive history archives and that of Lucas Richert focusing on the historicisation and investigation of psychiatric practices and radicalism in mental health. Redlinski and Wrighton's talk also raised the issues of technology and accessibility.

Besides the theme of collections, to which half the panel sessions were devoted, one panel examined collection management. The importance of looking at how collections are managed emerges from the 'acknowledgement that invisible, intellectual structures actually have a relationship to the material world of knowledge construction'.[17] During his contribution, Gregory Toth looked closely at metadata and how libraries must deal with discriminatory taxonomies. Importantly, he noted that card catalogue users need to be able to find themselves on first try. Alycia Sellie and Julio Cazzasa also gave papers for this panel, both of which are included in this volume. In brief, Cazzasa's was about a cataloguer's creativity in cataloguing radical

14 Gina Schlesselman-Tarango, 'Introduction' and Todd Honma, 'Foreword', *Topographies of Whiteness: Mapping Whiteness in Library and Information Science* (Sacramento, CA: Library Juice Press, 2017), ix–xiv at xi and 1–28 at 6.

15 Ian Beilin, 'The Academic Research Library's White Past and Present', *Topographies of Whiteness: Mapping Whiteness in Library and Information Science* (Sacramento, CA: Library Juice Press, 2017), 79–98 at 80.

16 Honma, xiii.

17 Emily Drabinski, 'Critical Art Librarianship Conference', published at Emily Drabinski, 25 May 2018. See www.emilydrabinski.com/critical-art-librarianship-conference/ (accessed 9 Aug. 2018).

collections while Sellie looked at a librarian's role in regard to various aspects of collections, from development to withdrawal. The final panel was about the people to be found in libraries and archives, from those entering the professions to readers in public and higher education (HE) libraries. Tamsin Bookey's talk about the Tower Hamlets Local History Library and Archives mentioned the demographic mismatch in population of Tower Hamlets and usage of the archives, which has led her to look at ways in which the service can be more representative of the community and widen participation to extend beyond the current dominant culture, that is, white people. She touched on the social model of disability and its application to archives, the importance of identifying barriers to archive use and dismantling them, opening employment opportunities to more diverse audiences and building equitable partnerships. The contributions of other speakers on that panel, Kirsty Fife, Hannah Louise Henthorn and Katherine Quinn, are included in this collection. Quinn considered radical librarianship in light of changes in UK HE institutions and Fife and Henthorn ended the day with an examination of diversity initiatives in the archives sector.

As expected, many ideas and concepts crossed the confines of the panels, with Toth's discussion of taxonomy providing further background to Britton's allusion to the fact that taxonomies often do not well reflect the radical content of zines. Sellie's encouragement of applying critical theory to library and information studies (LIS) squared well with the last panel's debates, in which Bookey, Quinn, Fife and Henthorn explored widening participation in libraries and archives for readerships and the information professions alike. Among other threads, funding was mentioned a few times, including by Redlinski and Bookey, although it may well be a topic for a future day of talks.

Questions followed the panel sessions, discussion continued during breaks and lunch, and Twitter reflected the enthusiasm evident in the room and coming from those who could not attend on the day. Just to choose a few ideas that caught the attention of the event's tweeters, many drew inspiration from Redlinski's call to get academics using collections in the classroom. Richert's question, raised in passing, concerning whether the promotion of radical collections increases their use by researchers, was tweeted and retweeted by several attendees. During Sellie's talk two ideas spread through the tweeters: the first supported the issues she raised concerning whiteness in libraries, and the second reflected the joy among information professionals that she believed the weeding of collections was not only important but potentially a radical act. Lastly, Richert's aside that historians must build relationships with librarians and archivists was warmly received!

The following conference contributors have graciously submitted their work to be published on this platform, providing a legacy of a day of discussions that aimed to contribute to ongoing conversations about the nature of collecting and collections in libraries and archives. Continuing along conference themes, the chapters in this volume are organised by the questions they seek to answer. Most of them answer more than one question so how they are organised is just as up for question as the issues examined during the conference. For example, Sellie's contribution is placed under the question 'what', but could just as easily address the questions of 'who' and 'what now'. Fife and Henthorn's paper, situated under 'what now' here, also very clearly addresses the question 'who'. The chapters that follow therefore cover multiple subjects and – to use library terminology – could easily be 'cross-referenced'.

The first chapter, which focuses on our question of 'who', is a case study about a librarian in Cork during the birth of the Irish Free State, later the Republic of Ireland. Mairéad Mooney's story about James Wilkinson, the librarian of Cork city's public library from 1892 until 1933, examines its children's collection and Wilkinson's development of it during a time of massive political and social change. The next two chapters explore, among other things, 'what' is in collections. Alycia Sellie's paper, 'Beyond the Left: documenting American racism in print periodicals at the Wisconsin Historical Society, and theorising (radical) collections today', raises a number of issues about collections and information professionals. Her work covers critical theory applied to LIS, addressing whiteness in libraries, and making it clear that inclusion and diversity within collections are not enough. Lucas Richert focuses on the use of archives from the researcher's perspective in his chapter, '"Mind meddling": exploring drugs and radical psychiatry in archives', answering the question of 'what'. His overview of his experiences in delving into radical psychiatry explores how information professionals' work in collecting, preserving and making materials available has had an impact on his research.

Julio Cazzasa's chapter, 'Cataloguing the radical material: an experience requiring a flexible approach', is the story of three collections and one cataloguer, giving insight into the cataloguing process and the issues that arise. His description of his work on these collections – all left wing but quite disparate, covering a wide subject area and languages – reveal the impact of a cataloguer's decisions and ideas. Following up on the question of 'how', Kirsty Fife and Hannah Louise Henthorn's contribution, 'Decentring qualification: a radical examination of archival employment possibilities', looking at the future of libraries, archives and the professions, asks 'what now?'. The authors look closely at the process of qualification for archivists. Their description of the costs involved in qualifying and gaining access to the archival professions demonstrates how that access is restricted, even at a time when collecting and engagement focus on diversity and inclusion. They also review the current system and propose new ways of gaining entry to the professions. Finally, Katherine Quinn's 'Enabling or envisioning politics of possibility? Examining the radical potential of academic libraries' breaks down the impact of current HE trends on libraries, then examines the Radical Librarians Collective and the Hive, Worcester, as forces that act against the marketisation of universities and libraries.

The Radical Collections conference provided a space to debate the issues of collection development, management and promotion, where professional ethics and futures could be discussed and experiences shared. Libraries and archives have long collected radical materials, but a re-examination of the information professions and all aspects of managing such collections is overdue – to encompass selection, appraisal and accession, through to organisation and classification, and including promotion and use. The conference and this volume have brought goals into focus which aim to widen access and ensure the future preservation of important but potentially marginalised collections and their use. These initiatives have formed part of many such discussions currently taking place which are trying to get to the root of collecting radically. To borrow from the call for papers, contributors to the conference and this book have demonstrated the importance of continuing to ask 'what now?'.

1. Radical or reactionary? James Wilkinson, Cork Public Library and identity in the Irish Free State

Mairéad Mooney

James Wilkinson was librarian of Cork city's public library from the inauguration of the service in 1892 until his retirement in 1933, stewarding it through a forty-year tenure which was characterised by major political and social change. Having commenced his post in Cork during the reign of Queen Victoria, Wilkinson's career was punctuated by the upheavals attendant on World War I, the War of Independence and the Irish Civil War. The War of Independence – also referred to as the Anglo-Irish War – was particularly significant for Wilkinson, as the purpose-built Carnegie Free Library became a casualty, a short-lived fifteen years after its opening, when crown forces set fire to Cork city on the night of 11 December 1920. The library premises, which included living quarters for Wilkinson and his family, and its stock of 14,000 volumes were destroyed.

It is thanks to Wilkinson's herculean efforts that a temporary library was established, followed by the construction of a superior purpose-built facility which opened in 1930. The accession record ledgers document the re-establishment of the library's collections, with the first title recorded on 6 February 1922, the month after the Anglo-Irish peace treaty had been ratified. Thus, the birth of the Irish Free State (later, the Republic of Ireland) converged with the re-birth of Cork Public Library (CPL).

It would therefore seem to have been a timely opportunity to assemble library collections representative of the new state's drive towards de-anglicisation, particularly the children's collection, given the perceived importance of the child as inheritor of the independent nation. However, analysis of the children's titles acquired by the library between 1922 and the outbreak of World War II demonstrates a surprising continuity with typical colonial period texts, largely maintaining the incontrovertible justice of imperial Britain's cultural and political superiority to other nations. Based on accession records evidence examined in their historical context, this chapter considers whether James Wilkinson, a Protestant Englishman, was a reactionary whose views were out of sympathy with postcolonial Ireland or, rather, a radical who recognised that children were not passive and uncritical assimilators of their recreational reading.

M. Mooney, 'Radical or reactionary? James Wilkinson, Cork Public Library and identity in the Irish Free State', in J. Landes and R. Espley (eds.), *Radical collections: re-examining the roots of collections, practices and information professions* (London: Senate House Library, 2018), pp. 9–21. License: CC-BY-NC-ND.

Librarians, as curators and mediators of reading material, had to contend with a culture of anxiety in relation to books and newspapers in the post-independence era. The Free State was engaged in a comprehensive programme to de-anglicise the new nation. Print was a crucial forum in which to project the superiority of the idealised Free State image of the wholesome Catholic Irish over their morally lax British neighbours. Social historian Anthony Keating traces this opposition to the apprehensions of 'religio-nationalist ideologues',[1] who feared that the population of Ireland had been adversely affected by the imposition of imperial rule, and who therefore demanded that corrupting external influences had to be minimised, to rehabilitate the spirituality of the people. British publications were thus frequently portrayed as a source of contamination, particularly for the young, upon whom the stability of the newly established state depended. Layman and cleric alike contributed to this rhetoric. The Archbishop of Tuam, in 1927, urged 'our Government to pass, with all haste such [censorship] legislation as will deliver our country from a dire evil which, if unchecked, will eat like a canker into the moral vitals of the brave sons and fair daughters of Erin.'[2] In 1929, a Limerick city councillor insisted that '[i]t was a well known fact … that young people borrowed pernicious books from one another, as a result of which their minds and general outlook were impaired' by what he termed 'the outpourings of hell'.[3] This reportedly 'well known fact' corroborates the archbishop's prediction, two years before, of an inevitable degeneracy overtaking young Irish Catholics, and this prognosis gained sufficient currency to galvanise some supporters into public newspaper burnings and activities which, in other contexts, would be considered criminal.

For instance, a representative of the Cork Angelic Warfare Association was prosecuted for larceny in 1927, as he and three other members had seized copies of British newspapers considered objectionable for their lurid reporting of crime and divorce cases.[4] Various religious-based lobby groups had been campaigning for amendment to the existing obscenity laws, which they regarded as insufficient and unfit for purpose. These pressure groups forced the justice minister to order an investigation, which resulted in a report produced by the dramatically named Committee on Evil Literature. The report validated the activists' assertions and prompted the introduction of a more draconian censorship legislation in 1929. The 'Angelic Warfare' court case was heard in March 1927, three months after the committee's report, and thus took place in a vacuum of sorts, as the revised legislation was not enacted until 1929. The state was obliged to prosecute for theft, and

1   'The uses and abuses of censorship: God, Ireland and the battle to extend censorship post 1929', *Estudios Irlandeses: Journal of Irish Studies* [online, 2014], 9: 67–79, at 68. See www.estudiosirlandeses.org/2014/02/the-uses-and-abuses-of-censorship-god-ireland-and-the-battle-to-extend-censorship-post-1929/ (accessed 12 Jun. 2018).
2   'The Lenten Pastorals', *The Connacht Tribune*, 5 Mar. 1927, p. 6.
3   'Outpourings of Hell', *The Limerick Leader*, 18 Feb. 1929, p. 3.
4   L.M. Cullen, *Eason & Son: a History* (Dublin: Eason, 1989), p. 267.

the defendant was found guilty, but was given a very lenient sentence. This reflected the prevailing mood in the court room that the police had been placed in the dilemma of having to neglect the greater crime of damage to public morality and under pressure to persecute the man who was generally perceived as the hero of the dispute. Since it was concerned with obscenity, the amended censorship legislation did not impact particularly on children's literature. Nonetheless, it was part of a nationalist discourse which sought to polarise Britain and Ireland, depicting Protestant Britain and its immoral publishing industry as the antithesis of Catholic Ireland, an outpost of purity endangered by its morally inferior neighbour.

The vulnerability of a librarian, perceived to be contravening the impetus to de-anglicise, is illustrated by the controversy that took place in County Mayo on the west coast of Ireland, and it is significant that James Wilkinson did not fall foul of similar accusations. In 1930, a political crisis erupted in Mayo which threatened to unseat the Cumann na nGaedhael government which had led the Irish Free State since British withdrawal in 1922. This crisis was not precipitated by the major issues the government of a fragile new state was confronting, such as the border with Northern Ireland, large-scale emigration and a lack of industrialisation. Rather, it was due to the seemingly parochial matter of appointing a county librarian. The appointment of Miss Letitia Dunbar Harrison led to a hostile reaction because, although an experienced librarian, she was Protestant, an objectionable quality which was compounded by her status as a graduate of Trinity College, Dublin. This sectarian bias needs to be understood in the context of the time. The Irish nationalist movement framed independence from Britain as a dialectic of Gaelic Ireland versus Anglo-Saxonised Ireland. The historian F.S.L. Lyons encapsulates what this translated to, in theory at least, in the early decades of the Irish Free State: 'Catholicism and Gaelicism, and the nationalism they nourished, were reacting primarily against England ... [i]t was English manners and morals, English influences, English Protestantism, English rules, that they sought to eradicate'.[5] In addition, the County Mayo region had suffered much, particularly during the Great Famine of the 1840s, and there was a residual suspicion of Protestant evangelism due to a number of Protestant-run famine-relief schemes where assistance to the starving was conditional on renouncing the Catholic faith for Protestantism.[6] Furthermore, Trinity College was seen as a Protestant institution whose graduates largely found opportunities within, and thus perpetuated, the British Empire.

Letitia Dunbar Harrison's appointment therefore offered an opportunity for the Fianna Fáil opposition party to undermine the government. The matter escalated to national attention. Provocative language was used: 'Miss Dunbar

5   In *Culture and Anarchy in Ireland* (Oxford: Oxford University Press, 1979), p. 82.
6   For discussion and further sources see Seán Stitt's article, 'GOD BE PRAISED! The roles and attitudes of Irish Protestants during the Potato Famine', *Insight Magazine: New Perspectives in Irish Studies* [Online], Association of Young Irish Archaeologists, (2). See http://homepage. eircom.net/~archaeology/two/famine.htm (accessed 13 Jun 2018).

Harrison was a graduate of Trinity College and as such must be imbued with West-British sentiments'; 'I object to Trinity College not because it's Protestant but because it is un-Irish. It is anti-Irish and anti-Catholic'; 'The Protestant ascendancy ... its venomous purposes of imposing its alien thought, its special standards of moral conduct, standards now publicly and palpably debased, on the Catholic people of this country'; 'When Miss Dunbar initially crosses the [River] Shannon she will not shed the scales of Anglicisation. She has been nurtured in the school of anti-nationalism.'[7] This language is dehumanising. Dunbar Harrison and, by association, Protestantism, which in turn was associated with Ireland's former colonial oppressor, was being portrayed in parliamentary debates and news accounts as monstrous and reptilian, and automatically hostile to the values of Mayo's Catholic population.[8]

The most suggestive comment was made by Eamon De Valera, leader of the Fianna Fáil party which was shortly to defeat the Cumann na nGaedheal government in the 1932 general election. Future prime minister De Valera declared that:

> [I]f it is a mere passive position of handing down books that are asked for, then the librarian has no particular duty for which religion should be regarded as a qualification, but if the librarian goes round to the homes of the people trying to interest them in books, sees the children in the schools and asks these children to bring home certain books, or asks what books their parents would like to read; if it is active work of a propagandist educational character – and I believe it must be such if it is to be of any value at all and worth the money spent on it – then I say the people of Mayo, in a county where ... over 98 per cent of the population is Catholic, are justified in insisting upon a Catholic librarian.[9]

These inflammatory remarks were less representative of public opinion than of stakeholders' manoeuvres to serve their own respective interests. The coverage of the matter in press and pulpit was less about any particular significance accorded to libraries and librarians than church and state posturing. The library committee opposed the ratification of Letitia Dunbar Harrison's appointment with a 10–2 majority, the county council opposed it 21–6. The government duly dissolved the council for failing to appoint Dunbar Harrison but a boycott of the library service followed, in which approximately one hundred – the majority – of the depots across the county no longer

---

7   Quoted in Pat Walsh *The Curious Case of the Mayo Librarian* (Cork: Mercier Press., 2009), pp. 63, 65, 69, 158. See also J.J. Lee's analysis in *Ireland, 1912–1985: Politics and Society* (Cambridge: Cambridge University Press, 1989), pp. 161–8, and Felicity Devlin's doctoral thesis, 'Brightening the countryside – the library service in rural Ireland, 1902–1935' (1990) at: http://eprints.maynoothuniversity.ie/5320/1/Felicity_Devlin_20140718135300.pdf (accessed 13 Jun. 2018).

8   Ibid.

9   Ibid., p. 176.

functioned. Such action might however, have been due to the Catholic clergy putting pressure on the local population to boycott the library service, rather than reflecting an authentic collective spirit of resistance to a non-Catholic librarian. Pat Walsh insists that it should not be assumed that the sentiment in Mayo represented public opinion country-wide.[10]

For Fianna Fáil, the stand-off was an opportune conflict between local and national governance, and the party leveraged it to destabilise the government's position. The Catholic Church, to which the governing party was obligated to maintain the popular vote, was also highly invested in proscribing reading matter that it regarded as potentially damaging to its followers. The Cumann na nGaedhal government, under whose public appointments criteria she had been legitimately offered the post, capitulated to the spiralling pressure. Dunbar Harrison was transferred from Mayo County Library to that at the Department of Defence. This is ironic, considering that if Dunbar Harrison was genuinely suspected of anti-Catholic sentiment and loyalty to the British crown, she was now surely far better positioned in the defence department to exploit opportunities to undermine Catholic Ireland.

Considering the furore caused even *before* Miss Dunbar Harrison took up her post, it is extraordinary that CPL's librarian, James Wilkinson, also a Protestant and, what is more, an Englishman, was not also subjected to similar professional discrediting. *The Catholic Mind* journal published an anonymous letter in March 1932 in which the writer bemoaned the alleged absence of a Catholic bible in the library holdings, which it attributed to Wilkinson's Protestantism.[11] While the adult collection is outside the scope of this discussion, only two bible-related titles are recorded in the children's holdings. Both were donations received in 1922 and neither was a Catholic publication. *The Catholic Mind* is blatant in its sectarian bias, claiming that '[n]o matter how well disposed the non-Catholic librarian may be, he cannot possibly be expected to get inside the Catholic mind'.[12] Public librarian, Pat Walsh, who has extensively researched the Mayo controversy, concluded that the accusation did not flourish because there was a lack of local support for *The Catholic Mind's* position.[13]

Why might that have been the case? As a contemporary library advocate observed, 'as nearly all our librarians are Catholics that is all to the good'.[14] A possible distinction between the Mayo and Cork situations is that James Wilkinson had been in situ for a considerable period (since October 1892), one which had straddled a time of major social upheaval, and that his commitment to the city's library service was publicly and manifestly attested by his successful endeavours to restore and enhance the service after the loss

10   Ibid., p. 200.
11   Ibid.
12   *Catholic Mind*, 3 (3), (1932), p. 56.
13   Walsh, *Curious Case*, p. 200.
14   Stephen Brown, *Libraries and Literature from a Catholic Standpoint* (Dublin: Browne and Nolan, 1937), p. 248.

of the Carnegie Library. His appeal for book donations galvanised a response nationally and internationally, with approximately 10,500 volumes donated by generous individuals and organisations. Wilkinson worked indefatigably to organise a temporary library and later a new, purpose-built facility, at a time when the city management was trying to cope with competing priorities associated with the rebuilding of the city centre.[15] This may explain why *The Catholic Mind*'s attempt to undermine Wilkinson's position as librarian failed to ignite a parallel controversy in Cork.

What is interesting is that the journal's stance could potentially have been borne out if the accession records for Wilkinson's term as librarian were selectively publicised; as mentioned, the only bible texts in the children's holdings were not Catholic publications. Furthermore, the children's collection continued to consist of predominantly British publications. Although a greater proportion of Irish-language, Irish-authored and Ireland-located texts began to be produced in the 1930s, and so contributed a greater number of domestic narratives to the collection, it remained overwhelmingly British and almost indistinguishable from a pre-independence collection. The reasons for this stasis are complex[16] but two significant factors should be noted. Firstly, as book historians Allen and Brown argue, Ireland was 'by 1939, scarcely free of an Imperial market that still dominated much of the world's economy'.[17] This prompted Irish publishers to be risk-averse, producing small print runs which in turn failed to generate much sales income for Irish authors and thereby curtailing the development of a thriving indigenous publishing industry. Additionally, the publications wing of the Free State's education department established an Irish language publication scheme, *An Gúm*, in 1925, to promote Irish speaking through the production of text books and recreational titles. The revival of the Irish language, which was in serious decline, was perceived as being dependent on fostering fluency in children, and thus the financially constrained new state prioritised investment in children's publications through the medium of Irish.

The obstacles to cultivating a domestic publishing output for Irish children was a source of frustration for Irish librarians of the period. The journal of the

---

15 See the library committee minute books and Wilkinson's correspondence as held in Cork City and County Archives; also, Thomas McCarthy's history of the library, *Rising from the Ashes: The Burning of Cork's Carnegie Library and the Rebuilding of its Collection* (Cork: Cork City Libraries, 2010). Also available at www.corkcitylibraries.ie/aboutus/librarypublications/ ashes.pdf (accessed 13 Jun. 2018).

16 For discussion of children's literature in Ireland in the early decades of the twentieth century, and the difficulties of establishing an indigenous publishing output, see Pat Donlon's chapter 'Books for Irish children', in Clare Hutton and Patrick Walsh (eds.) *The Oxford History of the Irish Book Volume: 5: The Irish Book in English 1891–2000* (Oxford: Oxford University Press, 2011), pp. 367–89. Nicholas Allen and Terence Brown's chapter,'Publishing after Partition, 1922–39' (pp. 70–88), and Allen's 'Reading revolutions, 1922–1939' (pp. 89–107), in the same volume, are also useful for an understanding of the literary landscape in the early Free State, though not specific to children's reading.

17 Allen and Brown,'Publishing after Partition, 1922–1939' (as above), p. 87.

Library Association of Ireland, from its re-launch in 1930 right through until World War I, documents a recurring exasperation with book selection for children. A rather acid comment was made by the Kilkenny librarian in the County Libraries Section Annual Report 1933–4:

> The usual lament of the county librarians on the dearth of suitable adventure books for children from 10–16 is also noticeable. The lament will soon become a national dirge on the part of county librarians, and I think it would be very wise if a few of our intellectual people in Ireland, whose brains are rusting for want of use, would sit down and write a few good school stories with an Irish background. I think it is time for our various literary academies to supply those idle brains with an incentive in the form of £20 or £30 for the best Irish school story.[18]

Other observations, though less blistering towards the intelligentsia, express similar sentiments. Irish public libraries were struggling to meet the demand for children's books in a post-independence publishing landscape that was generating far too few books intended for a young Irish readership, a state of affairs that did not reconcile with the de-anglicisation impetus.

Therefore, many of the texts in the children's collection at Cork's public library seem, from a twenty-first century perspective, ideologically incompatible with the vision of a Gaelic Ireland to which the state aspired. When compounded with the sensitivities regarding the public's reading consumption and the necessity to superintend the future citizen through the regulation of the child, the incongruity is even more pronounced. For example, Ethna Carbery's *In the Celtic Past* (originally published in 1904)[19] and T.B. Walters's *Charles T. Studd: Cricketer and Missionary* (1930)[20] were documented in the accession records on 5 and 10 December 1930 respectively. Garry Holohan, a member of the Fianna (an Irish nationalist equivalent of the British Boy Scouts) and later a member of the Irish Republican Brotherhood, attributes his republican radicalisation to reading the poetry of Ethna Carbery.[21] In contrast, cricket is perceived as a quintessentially English sport, and while Catholic missionaries were supported and admired, Protestant evangelism was regarded with suspicion.

18 County Libraries Section Annual Report, 1933–34, *An Leabharlann*, 5 (1), p. 22.
19 Carbery (A. J. MacManus), *In the Celtic Past* (Dublin: Talbot Press, undated).
20 Walters, *Charles T. Studd: Cricketer and Missionary* (London: Epworth, 1930).
21 Quoted in Marie Hay, 'An Irish nationalist adolescence: Na Fianna Éireann, 1909–23', in Catherine Cox and Susannah Riordan (eds.) *Adolescence in Modern Irish History* (Basingstoke: Palgrave Macmillan, 2015), pp. 103–28 at p. 122.

Our Empire Story: Stories of India and the Greater Colonies by H.E. Marshall[22] (*c*.1908) was recorded on 30 June 1931. This is a self-congratulatory celebration of the origins and expansion of the British empire. Marshall does acknowledge that imperial history is not an entirely glorious narrative: 'The stories are not all bright. How should they be? We have made mistakes, we have been checked here, we have stumbled there'.[23] However, the author defuses any more critical reflection on the legacy of colonial damage: 'We may own it without shame, perhaps almost without sorrow, and still love our Empire and its builders' [ibid]. Mrs Stephen Gwynn's *Stories from Irish History* (1904)[24] was documented seven months later. Joost Augusteijn reports that this was one of two texts singled out for attention in a backlash against the teaching of Irish history, which was considered to have been a major contributing factor to the 1916 Easter Rising.[25] Mrs Gwynn articulated a counter-narrative to Marshall's panegyric to imperial Britain, a text much more in sympathy with Free State sentiment in 1932. One of the tensions which public librarians had to negotiate was the one between their role in educating and elevating members' reading tastes and the fact that since libraries were rate-supported their members felt entitled to be supplied with the reading material they desired. It is surely unlikely that Marshall's text would have fallen within the desirable category a mere decade after independence from Britain.

While adventure stories – including those by authors who have been identified as presenting a pro-imperial ideology in their works (G.A. Henty, W.H.G. Kingston, W.E. Johns and Charles Kingsley, for example) – do occupy a significant proportion of the collection, the school story genre for both boys and girls is the most prolific. Also, the school settings are predominantly the exclusive type of private educational establishment, generally with an English setting, the 'venerable pile'[26] in which constructions of manhood are endorsed or criticised. Cork Public Library held F.W. Farrar's *Eric*,[27] and Thomas Hughes' *Tom Brown's School Days*,[28] regarded as founding texts of the public school story genre. While both of these titles were originally acquired as donations to stock subsequent to the 1920 fire, further copies of Hughes' text were added to stock in 1930 and 1936, after the library was fully operational once more and based in a new, purpose-built facility. The genre promoted the

22   Marshall, *Our Empire Story: Stories of India and the Greater Colonies* (T.C and E. C Jack, p. viii, n13, undated). 1908 edition available from: https://archive.org/details/cu31924087978601 (accessed 18 Jun. 2018).

23   Ibid., p. viii.

24   *Stories from Irish History* (Dublin, Belfast, Cork, Waterford: Browne and Nolan, undated).

25   Joost Augusteijn, 'Motivation: why did they fight for Ireland? The motivation of volunteers in the Revolution', in Augusteijn (ed.) *The Irish Revolution, 1913–1923* (Basingstoke, Houndmills; New York, NY: Palgrave, pp. 103–20 at p. 114.

26   Frank O'Connor, 'The Idealist', in *The Stories of Frank O'Connor* (London: Hamish Hamilton, 1953), p. 43.

27   W.F. Farrar, *Eric, or, Little by Little* (London: Ward, Lock & Co, undated).

28   *Tom Brown's School Days* (London: Macmillan, 1898).

qualities befitting those public schoolboys who would later swell the ranks of those directing the extension and administration of the British empire; the empire from which the Free State had so recently extracted itself after years of guerrilla warfare and a highly divisive civil war.

In 1936, D. Billington[29] advised aspiring writers of children's literature that '[s]tories of war, like the old romances of Henty and other writers, are for the present out of favour. If boys like them, their parents and teachers do not.'[30] The reverse appears to be true of CPL in the same timeframe, as forty-seven Henty books were in the holdings and a batch of eleven titles was entered in the accession records on 7 July 1932. Based on Billington's analysis, Wilkinson's provision of the Henty titles aligns him with the indiscriminate boy readers rather than the critical adult stakeholders made up of teachers and parents. In their roles as mediators of suitable reading material for Irish children, post-independence public librarians were perceived as contributing to the stability of the state through a national project to cultivate desirable future citizens.[31] Henty's continued acquisition of texts which fulsomely lauded Britain's imperial conquests – for example, *With Kitchener in the Soudan* and *With Clive in India*[32] – does on the face of it raise questions as to Wilkinson's suitability as a librarian in post-independence Ireland. Alternatively, Wilkinson may have shared the opinion of Kimberley Reynolds, professor of children's literature, that Henty's texts promoted the self-advancement of boys and young men 'in order to support dependant relations and to take on civic responsibilities.'[33] As the new state was concerned with fostering a sense of citizenship, these novels may have been considered appropriate reading material in terms of their citizenly underpinnings rather than their imperial framework.

Such a view may also explain the addition to the children's collection of *The Model Citizen: a Simple Exposition of Civic Rights and Duties and a Descriptive*

---

29 Likely to have been Dick Billington, a Frederick Warne employee who was made director of children's literature in 1940, and managing director soon afterwards. My thanks to Richard Espley for alerting me to this.

30 D. Billington, *Hints on Writing Juvenile Literature* (London: Warne, 1936), p. 21.

31 For instance, James Wilkinson's successor, Eugene Carberry, commented in 1935 that 'the Public Library can be a very powerful instrument for the training of the good citizen'. See *An Leabharlann*, Dec. 1935 5/2 61. That sentiment recurs throughout the narrative timeframe in the journal of the Librarian Association of Ireland. It is echoed in contemporary library policy: in 2013 the Department of the Environment, Community and Local Government's library strategy stated that '[c]hildhood reading is critical for both skills development and play. There are strong associations between functional illiteracy and poverty, crime, ill-health and community strife'. See Department of the Environment, Community and Local Government, *Opportunities for All: the Public Library as a Catalyst for Economic, Social and Cultural Development. A Strategy for Public Libraries 2013–2017* (Dublin: Department of the Environment, Community and Local Government, 2013), p. 21. Available at: www.lgma.ie/sites/default/files/public_libraries_strategy_2013_2017.pdf (accessed 18 Jun. 2018).

32 G.A. Henty, *With Clive in India, or, The Beginnings of an Empire* and *With Kitchener in the Soudan, a story of Atbara and Omdurman* (both Glasgow, London: Blackie, undated).

33 Kimberley Reynolds, *Girls Only? Gender and Popular Children's Fiction in Britain, 1880–1910* (Hemel Hempstead: Harvester Wheatsheaf, 1991), p. 72.

Account of British Institutions Local, National and Imperial (1924 edition).[34] The title, and the many rather jingoistic effusions within the text itself, make this choice seem anachronistic. The War of Independence (1919–21) and Irish Civil War (1922–3) were still fresh and painful memories when Wilkinson recorded this addition to stock in December 1924. The narrator's observation that '[w]hen people have government forced upon them without any choice, we call it tyranny or despotic government' is succeeded by the assertion that 'British government is now the admiration and model of the world'. The omission of any recognition that the globally admired model of British governance had itself enforced 'despotic government' on other nations is likely to have been unfavourably received by Irish nationalist readers. However, the Free State government did, in fact, retain much of the British governmental and administrative model after independence and so this volume would have been quite useful as guide for illustrating to Irish children the mechanics of national management. The Earl of Meath's foreword to the 1907 edition indicates that an awareness of citizenship had not been fostered in British children:

> Too little care has been taken in the past to train the rising generation of Britons in those virtues which tend towards the growth of good Citizenship, and to impart to them the knowledge which shall enable them, when they grow up, to appreciate, to preserve, and to make the best use of those free institutions which are the glory of the British Empire.[35]

Citizenship was also a new concept in the Free State. It may be argued that Wilkinson recognised the continued convergence between British and Free State administration, and that Irish children were capable of exercising a critical distance between books vaunting imperial Britain and their own allegiance to the Irish Free State.

Regardless of present-day interpretations of the rationale governing acquisitions in the 1920s and 30s, it must be remembered that the librarian was not solely responsible for selecting the texts. The recommendations of CPL's library committee took precedence, though in practice a books committee sub-group consisting of Wilkinson and a Catholic priest library committee member managed book selections. Committee members were appointed by Cork City Council and comprised councillors, clerics, and lay representatives. The importance of soliciting church support in matters of civic administration may be inferred from the fact that Rev. Fr. Kiely (later Canon) occupied the position of chair for ten of the seventeen years that he was a member. The committee's minute books do, however, record that matters pertaining to the withdrawal of inappropriate titles or complaints from the public concerning specific texts were noted, and so it cannot be concluded that such operational

---

34 H. Osman Newland and T. Hunter Donald, *The Model Citizen* (as above) (London: Pitman, 1907), p. 20, available at: https://archive.org/details/McGillLibrary-108902-60 (accessed 18 Jun. 2018).

35 Ibid., p. 3.

matters were discharged without committee input. A board of city councillors and clerical representatives thereby officially, through their committee deputies, endorsed these seemingly incongruous stock choices. Hence, despite the public discourse of de-anglicisation, these titles were not thought to be detrimental to post-independence children and the development of their civic responsibilities. This chapter now considers the circumstances and influences which may have contributed to the approbation of titles.

Father Stephen Brown (1881–1962) was a Jesuit priest and librarian, and a founder of the librarianship training course in Dublin. He was a frequent contributor to the dialogue on public reading, especially in relation to children's reading. He recognised the power of book collections as potentially 'social and intellectual dynamite; or a laboratory of corrosive and corrupting suggestion'.[36] Brown offers a pragmatic rationale for the continued practice of stocking English children's literature in Irish children's libraries:

> Now let me explain why Irish children – and grown-ups, too, for that matter – are at a special disadvantage in this matter of books as compared with the children of most other countries. In the first place there is what I may call our literary dependence on another country whose ways, appreciations of things, and general outlook are very different from ours, and yet whose language, whether we like it or not, is the same as that of most of us. Its literature, vastly more abundant than what we can produce, is always at our disposal, and, of course, we are not going to be so foolish as to neglect what is good in it - at least till we have something to take its place.[37]

Essentially, literature, like any other commodity, is implicated in the economics of supply and demand. Hence it was necessary for the Free State, though celebrating its political independence from Britain, to continue to exist in a literary ecosystem which largely uncritically re-inscribed colonial Britain and its culture as the norm, and to which Ireland was peripheral. Brown rationalises this unsatisfactory situation by presenting it as a temporary situation and that English literature is merely substitutive for the national children's literature that will displace it in time.

However, Brown is clearly conscious that projecting too positive a picture of the richness of English children's literature may actually undermine the momentum to produce an Irish canon of children's writing. He appeals to his adult readers' charged memories of colonial Ireland in order to stimulate resistance to such a possibility:

> [M]any of us would not like our boys and girls to be brought up solely in the atmosphere of what is, after all, a foreign literature, unless we are content with the ideal of the early National schools

---

36   See 'On book selection', *An Leabharlann*, 1 (1), Jun. 1930, p. 5.
37   *Irish Story-Books for Boys and Girls* (Dublin: Office of the Irish Messenger, 1922), p. 4.

> – the 'happy British child'. Moreover, the vast bulk of literature
> in English is written by non-Catholics and for non-Catholics,
> whether or not it be distinctively Protestant in character (ibid.).

Brown is alluding to the pre-independence national schools' curriculum which included a poem expressing gratitude for the good fortune of having been born 'a happy British child'. Of English school stories, Brown admits that 'many, if not most, of these school stories are morally healthy in tone, and yet...'[38] The ellipsis is revealing: Brown is unable to articulate a specific objection to these narratives. As he recognises, they are not incompatible with Catholic morality. Possibly what is objectionable is that, as Cork writer Daniel Corkery lamented, post-independence Ireland continued to filter its self-image through an English lens.[39]

As mentioned, sport was also politically charged. A year after the establishment of the Gaelic League, which promoted the de-anglicisation of Ireland, the Gaelic Athletic Association (GAA) was founded in 1894 for the purpose of promoting Irish sports. Rugby and cricket were considered 'foreign' sports and as such could not be played in GAA stadia. However, the memoirs of Bill Hammond, who grew up in a deprived area of working-class Cork in the 1930s, betrays no consciousness of the ideological freighting of sports. The author recalls that '[p]laying Cricket, when "Hammond" came in to bat, and having the same surname as the famous Cricketer, a lot was expected of me'.[40] Cricket is presented as popular with local children, and also as having a widespread national following. Therefore, CPL's purchase in November 1935 of *First Principles of Cricket*, a Boys' Own Paper publication, as well as the above-mentioned *Charles T. Studd: Cricketer and Missionary*, may be less a continued subscription to imperial Britain's prescription of children's literature than an apolitical, entirely pragmatic purchase of an instruction guide for a popular local sport.

Another text with explicitly imperialist overtones is Daniel Defoe's *Robinson Crusoe*. The Cork Free Library records catalogue published that it was held in the children's collection from at least 1896, and was acquired for the city's public library six times between 1922 and 1939, as were a number of Robinsonades, a sub-genre of the Crusoe text. In 1912, James Joyce expressed the imperialist reception of Crusoe, in whom he saw 'the true symbol of the British conquest' in these terms: 'He is the true prototype of the British colonist, as Friday (the faithful savage who arrives one ill-starred day) is the symbol of the subject race. All the Anglo-Saxon soul is in Crusoe'.[41] Richard Phillips, discussing attempts in the 1970s to rehabilitate perceived

---

38 'II – Irish fiction for boys', *Studies: an Irish Quarterly Review of Letters Philosophy and Science* (7) Dec. 1918, pp. 665–70 at p. 666.

39 'Live libraries", *An Leabharlann*, Cork Conference supplementary no., Dec. 1933, pp. 141–8.

40 *Footsteps on Blarney Street* (Cork: Lithopress, 1992), p. 23.

41 'Realism and idealism in English Literature (Daniel Defoe and William Blake)', in Kevin Barry (ed.), *Occasional, Critical and Political Writing* (Oxford: Oxford University Press, 2000), pp.163–82 at p. 174.

racism in children's literature, argues that the interpretation of narratives by child readers cannot be pre-determined and observes that 'as readers from Karl Marx to Virginia Woolf, and from Jean-Jacques Rousseau to countless ordinary people have shown, *Robinson Crusoe* can be read as a colonial tale, but alternatively it can be read as a critique of established religion, a capitalist utopia, a story of natural man and so on'.[42] Thus, Crusoe's self-sufficiency, his piety, and his cultivation and civilisation of an island, may have appealed to post-independence Irish readers as an inspiring text for the embryonic Free State, resonating with the nationalist ideal of restoring a purified and autonomous pre-colonial island.

It should not be assumed, therefore, that the titles stocked in Cork's public library in the post-revolutionary period conflicted with the Free State ideology of a culturally distinctive Gaelic Ireland. Regrettably, primary sources containing the responses of child readers of the period are few. James Smith Allen notes that 'literature was recreated by historical audiences, and may have been recreated in a fashion quite unlike anything envisioned by the author or the critic'.[43] Children who read these books as Ireland embarked on a process of establishing a postcolonial identity may have engaged with these texts in ways which transformed or defused apparently imperialist or culturally exclusive narratives. So, was James Wilkinson a radical or a reactionary? In answer, I will cannibalise a line from the poet W.B. Yeats: 'How can we know the dancer from the dance?'[44] – How can we know the collector from the collection? In this case, we cannot, as Wilkinson was not exclusively responsible for the holdings, nor can the processes of book selection that were in operation be tracked. What is more, the native publishing industry of English-language material for children did not begin to produce a sizeable body of output until the 1980s, so the predominance of British publications in the children's collection was simply a consequence of a dearth of alternatives.

What distinguishes James Wilkinson's career is his indomitable efforts to ensure the restoration of a lost library, recognising that even in a time of war, the value of libraries transcends political and geographical divisions. This is framed in the request for donations which the library committee issued in the aftermath of the burning: 'we confidently appeal to those who without distinction of creed, race or class, wish to help in this humanitarian and educational reparation',[45] a confidence not misplaced, as the thousands of donated texts attest. Whether radical, reactionary or neither, James Wilkinson was a champion of the library service in Cork at a time when radical and reactionary activity was transforming the island of Ireland.

42 'Politics of reading; decolonising children's geographies', *Cultural Geographies*, 8 (2) (2001): 125–50 at p. 144.
43 Qouted in Jonathan Rose, 'Rereading the English common reader: a preface to a history of audiences', in David Finkelstein and Alistair McCleery (eds.), *The Book History Reader*, second edn. (London: Routledge, 2006), pp. 424–39 at p. 429.
44 'Among school children'.
45 McCarthy, *Rising from the Ashes*, p. 16.

2. Beyond the Left: documenting American racism in print periodicals at the Wisconsin Historical Society, and theorising (radical) collections today

Alycia Sellie

Dear Well-Meaning White People Who Want Nothing to do with Alt-Right: We, people of color, cannot carry this burden. You must engage.[1]

Jose Antonio Vargas

White supremacy in the United States is a central organizing principle of social life rather than merely an isolated social movement.[2]

Jessie Daniels

...this paper is a call to action: it is a plea for practicing archivists to work actively and diligently against white supremacist bias by documenting white supremacist violence against Black Americans.[3]

Tonia Sutherland

IIn 2005 or thereabouts, while working at the Wisconsin Historical Society (WHS), I emailed an editor to enquire about a recent publication. I had discovered a print newsletter that had been published for some time, but which the WHS did not yet hold. I hadn't expected a response because the organisation's website looked outdated and I couldn't tell whether it was being maintained. Yet I got a quick and enthusiastic reply. The editor was happy to hear from me, and had good news: not only would they be able to send the newsletters, but because members of their group lived nearby in the next county, they would be able to get the issues to us immediately.

This encounter stuck in my mind because the editor with whom I was corresponding was an unabashed white supremacist and his organisation was tied to the Ku Klux Klan. The fact that it had members in a nearby location

---

1   Jose Antonio Vargas, Twitter post, 12 Aug. 2017, 12:53 am. https://twitter.com/joseiswriting/status/896233228935221248 (accessed 19 Jun. 2018).

2   Jessie Daniels, *White Lies: Race, Class, Gender and Sexuality in White Supremacist Discourse* (New York, NY: Routledge, 1997), p. 11.

3   Tonia Sutherland, 'Archival amnesty: in search of black American transitional restorative justice', *Journal of Critical Library and Information Studies*, 1 (2) (2017): 1–22 at 3. See http://dx.doi.org/10.24242/jclis.v1i2.42 (accessed 19 Jun. 2018).

A. Sellie, 'Beyond the Left: documenting American racism in print periodicals at the Wisconsin Historical Society, and theorising (radical) collections today', in J. Landes and R. Espley (eds.), *Radical collections: re-examining the roots of collections, practices and information professions* (London: Senate House Library, 2018), pp. 23–34. License: CC-BY-SA..

was a chilling disappointment.[4] Almost a decade later, I cannot remember the title of the publication, although I am still haunted by the correspondence. I cannot easily work backwards to figure out which title it was, either: the WHS currently holds thirty-seven serial titles under the subject heading 'Ku Klux Klan — Periodicals', the majority of which are written not by those studying white supremacy, but by those who actively uphold or represent white hate.[5]

As a white woman raised in a working-class family in the Midwest, I was aware of the ways in which white people express fear.[6] I was also aware of hate groups — there had been times when racist literature was literally in the air. I distinctly remember the haunting experience of unfolding a crumpled flyer that had blown down my street when the realisation hit me that this method of distribution required those effecting it to live in close proximity to my home (much like how I felt at the WHS when I realised groups like this were organising nearby). My husband's parents likewise found literature on their lawn condemning interracial marriages such as theirs and discovered that their tyres had been slashed. This was not that long ago; the late 1980s and 1990s.

I've thought about this chapter and what I might say in it now that with every passing day in America we live with a white supremacist as president.[7] Headlines have been distracting my attention from what I originally presented at the Radical Collections conference; it's hard to know which conversations might still feel relevant when so much has been discussed this year about race and hatred in America. The Racial Imaginary website, an 'interdisciplinary cultural laboratory', founded by poet Claudia Rankine, approaches the subject as follows:

> The Institute begins with a focus on whiteness because we believe that in our current moment whiteness is freshly articulated: the volume on whiteness has been turned up. Whiteness as a source of unquestioned power, and as a 'bloc', feels itself to be endangered even as it retains its hold on power. Given that the concept of racial hierarchy is a strategy employed

4   See the full list of active groups affiliated with the Ku Klux Klan, currently tracked by the Southern Poverty Law Center, here: www.splcenter.org/fighting-hate/extremist-files/ideology/ku-klux-klan (accessed 19 Jun. 2018).

5   If I had to guess it might have been *The Flame*, out of Dayton, Ohio, because I distinctly remember the publication's headquarters being located in the northern US.

6   24/7 Wall Street has named Minnesota and Wisconsin — the two states I lived in up to the time I worked at the WHS — as the worst states for the quality of life of African Americans in its ranking of such factors as homeownership, incarceration rates and unemployment: http://247wallst.com/special-report/2016/12/08/worst-states-for-black-americans-3/4/ (accessed 19 Jun. 2018).

7   As Ta-Nehisi Coates writes, Trump's 'ideology is white supremacy, in all its truculent and sanctimonious power.' See Coates, '"The first white president: the foundation of Donald Trump's presidency is the negation of Barack Obama's legacy', *The Atlantic*, Oct. 2017, www.theatlantic.com/magazine/archive/2017/10/the-first-white-president-ta-nehisi-coates/537909/ (accessed 19 Jun. 2018)

to support white dominance, whiteness is an important aspect of any conversation about race. We begin here in order to make visible that which has been intentionally presented as inevitable so that we can move forward into more revelatory conversations about race. Our first project questions what can be made when we investigate, evade, beset and call out bloc-whiteness.[8]

As one of the most dangerous issues so often ignored, whiteness is part of what I would like to consider here. Or, echoing Michelle Caswell's work with library and information science (LIS) students, I will focus on 'identifying and dismantling' white supremacy in archives and libraries.[9] I am mindful or even wary of my own position in writing this chapter.[10] As a cis white heterosexual woman in a field filled with people like me, my desire is to confront whiteness and to use it to interrogate the past, or to better see the present. It feels precarious to suggest that collecting outright racist work might be part of anti-racist activism. But I am more concerned about not making this suggestion than making it; I worry that when librarians and archivists think about radical collections and leave out the terrors of the right, we (or the majority white people working in LIS) perpetuate structures of white power.

Although whiteness has been studied outside of LIS for some time, librarians and archivists are now beginning to write about its influence on the field, and the ways in which this concept can function in terms of power and culture.[11] Todd Honma, by way of George Lipsitz, describes whiteness as 'a socio-cultural category constantly created and recreated as a way to uphold the unequal distribution of wealth, power, and opportunity.'[12] Honma also describes how normalised the hegemonic hold of whiteness has become, and states that 'what counts as "universal" knowledge is an unquestioned and unacknowledged white perspective.' While dominant, whiteness is often

---

8   See 'About', The Racial Imaginary, https://theracialimaginary.org/about (accessed 19 Jun. 2018).

9   Michelle Caswell, 'Teaching to dismantle white supremacy in archives', The Library Quarterly, 87 (3) (8 Jun. 2017): 222–35. See https://doi.org/10.1086/692299 (accessed 19 Jun. 2018).

10 Sociologist Jessie Daniels recently wrote a blog post, 'How naming my family's white supremacy led me to change my own name', for Entropy, 7 Sep. 2017, available at: https://entropymag.org/name-tags-5-how-naming-my-familys-white-supremacy-led-me-to-change-my-own-name/ (accessed 19 Jun. 2018). She made that decision after discovering that her grandfather had been a member of the Ku Klux Klan. Wanting to completely separate herself from this history, while also studying white hate for her dissertation, her 'waking nightmare was that someone would see me as one of those Night Riders, rather than their adversary.' Daniels' worry speaks to my thoughts about publishing this chapter, where I have worried over arguing to preserve the very things I most wish did not exist.

11 Including even a full monograph, edited by Gina Schlesselman-Tarango, Topographies of Whiteness: Mapping Whiteness in Library and Information Science (Duluth, MN: Library Juice Press, 2017).

12 Todd Honma, 'Trippin' over the color line: the invisibility of race in library and information studies', InterActions: UCLA Journal of Education and Information Studies 1 (2) (2005): 5.

described as an elusive subject, one that 'never has to speak its name.'[13] Gina Schlesselman-Tarango writes: 'Because of its insistence on not naming itself, whiteness largely remains invisible (especially, it has been argued, by white subjects).'[14] So much of the conversation in LIS echoes the work of the broader Black Lives Matter movement and what the Racial Imaginary describes as making visible that which has been assumed inevitable, that which went unidentified and unquestioned.

This chapter merges what I experienced in developing collections at the WHS with new scholarship on anti-racism and interrogations of whiteness in library and information studies (LIS).[15] This is a personal exploration reconciling the whiteness of our profession with work that proposes breaks from the domination of whiteness.

Collecting newspapers and periodicals

During my time at the WHS its collections provided me with an eye-opening education in American culture. What I now think of as a true entry into American studies involved reading periodicals by folks with hobbies like brick-collecting, trade publications by cattle farmers, work written in prisons, and periodicals by and for many groups arguing for equality and liberation. In the newspapers and periodicals collection, the self-published, small run and radical print publications contain a spectrum of ideas within which the vastness of opinion is hard to summarise.[16]

Beyond that content, the WHS's collection development practices were radical. Although official policies were left loose, the librarian of the newspapers and periodicals section, James P. Danky, used a number of approaches when deciding what to add to it.[17] Those approaches have influenced my thinking in this chapter as well as my understanding of what it means to be a librarian working today. One of Danky's collection development methods sought to be entirely comprehensive; the WHS aimed to gather together every print serial publication produced within the state of Wisconsin. To this end,

---

13 Ibid., p. 15.

14 Gina Schlesselman-Tarango, 'The legacy of Lady Bountiful: white women in the library', *Library Trends*, 64 (4) (13 Sep. 2016): 667–86 at 669. See https://doi.org/10.1353/lib.2016.0015 (accessed 19 Jun. 2018).

15 I should also make it clear that this chapter is really focused on bringing together print publications for permanent collections rather than how hate groups use the internet, which feels like a very different conversation. For more on studying racism online, see: Jessie Daniels, *Cyber Racism: White Supremacy Online and the New Attack on Civil Rights* (New York, NY: Rowman & Littlefield, 2009) and Safiya Noble, *Algorithms of Oppression: How Search Engines Reinforce Racism* (New York, NY: NYU Press, 2018).

16 The WHS holds the second-largest collection of newspapers in the US, after the Library of Congress. While I worked there, the newspapers and periodicals section held 9,000 active subscriptions.

17 There was sufficient interest in Danky's diverse collecting practices to devote an entire issue of *Library Trends* to it. See *Library Trends*, 56 (3).

Danky encouraged all producers of a printed work to bring or send a copy to the WHS. He suggested to high school students of zines that they make their own, and bring a copy to the WHS to be catalogued and preserved. He collected political pamphlets on the fly on the mall outside the WHS. He used an inter-library mail system to allow publishers in corners of the state to send materials to him without paying for postage.

Another significant collection area was harder to define. These were items I often heard referred to as 'unique to OCLC',[18] or materials that no other library had yet catalogued in WorldCat.[19] These titles were grout and mortar; they filled in the spaces left by other libraries and archives. In adding these works, Danky was working on the larger scale of what had not yet been collected, searching against all library holdings in the United States. Much of what I learned from Danky in this practice was the importance of questioning standard library practices, or specifically trying to see the negative space left behind by other libraries.[20] Tactics for doing this work are encapsulated well in this story where Danky discovered barricades between the public library and the Haitian community in Miami. Here he describes his visit there:

> I asked the library worker at the desk if she could tell me where I might find a listing of Haitian-American periodicals. She said there weren't any but I could try Thomas' Register. Since I had already subscribed to 3 titles from Miami while in Wisconsin, I knew this was not true … Deflated but not defeated, we drove 125 feet past the [library's] intersection and found the store [suggested by a local cab driver] where I bought 27 new titles while enjoying Haitian music videos played at full volume. Now 125 feet may not seem like much, but it was an insurmountable barrier between the public library and the surrounding community.[21]

Danky was constantly working to bridge that 125-foot gap between what people read in the course of their lives and what they found on library shelves.

18 Online Computer Library Center.

19 Cataloguing statistics for the WHS from 2002 to 2006 show that 72% of the items added to the collection required original cataloguing, or were not already held by another institution. Maija Salo-Cravens, email to the author, 2–6 Mar. 2017.

20 I often think about the difference between what is held in the lobby of our libraries v. what is preserved in our collections via this quote from Danky: 'When you approach the security gates at the Madison, Wisconsin Public Library you encounter a large number of free distribution newspapers and magazines: shelter titles describing renting and real estate options; tabloid aimed at youth, especially music-related; a general-purpose alternative newsweekly; most wonderfully, the uncensored, satirical sheet titled *The Onion*; and small-format weeklies aimed at the Latino and Black communities … [these] publication[s], like so many, never made it past those security barriers. A wonderful example of librarians as gatekeepers.' Taken from his chapter, 'Libraries: they would have been a good idea', in Sanford Berman and James Danky (eds.) *Alternative Library Literature 1996–1997* (Jefferson, NC: Smallwood Press, 1998), pp. 3–6 at p. 5.

21 Ibid., p. 4.

He delighted in finding new and surprising materials, and paving a way not just for people to read them in Wisconsin but for other libraries to likewise subscribe (and copy-catalogue these Haitian-American titles after the WHS added them to WorldCat).

Both of these approaches – comprehensive local collecting and working into the empty spaces left by other collections – often brought us circling familiar realms and repeatedly adding work that it was clear our fellow librarians found challenging such as unpolished and impolite work about sex, race, religion, or other topics that some might be uncomfortable in presenting to the public.

The Ron Paul Freedom Report

Take the *Ron Paul Freedom Report*. What I remember of this publication was that the title changed frequently. Yet Ron Paul's name always stayed emblazoned across the top of each newsletter in a large, bold header. Over the years it ranged from *Ron Paul's Freedom Report* to *Ron Paul Political Report* and *The Ron Paul Survival Report*. I remember feeling confused when I held the newsletter – surviving *what*, exactly? The pieces were jumbled, the language was difficult to understand, but identifiably paranoid, hateful. Yet within the realm of materials collected at the WHS, it wasn't unusual: it sat within a spectrum of right-wing publications that seemed utterly inaccessible unless you were part of a very specific network.

During the run up to the 2008 US presidential elections, journalist James Kirchick wanted to write about Ron Paul's life before he became a candidate for president. Kirchick's enquiries led him to discover that Paul had had a long relationship with newsletter publishing:

> In the age before blogs, newsletters occupied a prominent place in right-wing political discourse. With the pages of mainstream political magazines typically off-limits to their views (*National Review* editor William F. Buckley having famously denounced the John Birch Society), hardline conservatives resorted to putting out their own, less glossy publications. These were often paranoid and rambling – dominated by talk of international banking conspiracies, the Trilateral Commission's plans for world government, and warnings about coming Armageddon – but some of them had wide and devoted audiences.

On the *Freedom Report* website, online issues only went back about a decade so Kirchick wrote, 'Finding the pre-1999 newsletters was no easy task, but I was able to track many of them down at the libraries of the University of Kansas and the Wisconsin Historical Society.'[22]

---

22   'Angry white man', *New Republic*, 8 Jan. 2008, https://newrepublic.com/article/61771/angry-white-man (accessed 19 Jun. 2018).

Kirchick published the findings he gleaned from these newsletters in a *New Republic* article of January 2008.[23] He summarised the contents as 'decades worth of obsession with conspiracies, sympathy for the right-wing militia movement, and deeply held bigotry against blacks, Jews, and gays'.[24] Although Paul has tried to distance himself from the newsletters and has claimed he was not responsible for writing any of the articles, the troubling content of these publications (and those headers bearing his name) have followed him throughout his political career.[25]

Although this example might not seem scalable – the practice of collecting hate tracts probably won't stand in the way of electing more bigoted men – it does show the potential for accountability processes. Collecting white hate also makes it possible for scholars to study the nuances within; according to sociologist Jessie Daniels, she would not have been able to research white supremacy for her dissertation and first book without spending time in the Klanwatch Archive at the Southern Poverty Law Center.[26] Reflecting on the Paul controversy, historian Chip Berlet praised the WHS collections and Danky, asking: 'Where else can you find a librarian who asks if the particular type of hate-group newsletter you are looking for is Ku Klux Klan, racial nationalist, neo-Nazi, Third Position, homophobic or Christian Identity?'[27] Although it may sound here like I'm arguing for all libraries or archives to collect and know these works, as Danky did, I am actually only arguing somewhat unscientifically for *enough*. Perhaps this takes the form of gathering everything local, including the problematic, as with Wisconsin publications at the WHS. Or perhaps the collecting I am arguing for works into those harsh silences and those places no other collections have explored – it is easy to find these missing collections, even among histories we all know and reference frequently.

Documenting white supremacist violence

In her recent article, 'Archival amnesty: in search of black American transitional and restorative justice', Tonia Sutherland summarises the material objects that were produced in the American South in relation to public lynchings, especially events large enough to be advertised or ticketed. Calling lynching a 'well-documented, pervasive, and ritual practice', Sutherland notes that 'despite a plethora of evidence … very little of this past is represented in American archives.' Although these material items created to commemorate those crimes still exist today, they aren't held in repositories. They 'proliferate

23   Ibid.

24   Ibid.

25   Andy Kroll, '10 extreme claims in Ron Paul's controversial newsletters', *Mother Jones*. See www.motherjones.com/politics/2012/01/ron-paul-newsletter-iowa-caucus-republican (accessed 19 Jun. 2018).

26   Jessie Daniels, *White Lies*.

27   Doug Moe, 'Historical Society reveals Ron Paul's incendiary past', *Capital Times*, 11 Jan. 2008. See www.freerepublic.com/focus/f-news/1951978/posts (accessed 19 Jun. 2018).

in online auctions and sales such as eBay', mirroring other auctions related to the black body in American history.[28]

Critiquing archival amnesty, Sutherland concludes that it was wholly intentional for early twentieth-century archivists to leave these 'records of trauma' out of official archives, and further,

> By failing to consistently collect this visual evidence as an intentional counter-narrative, American archives have effectively created a master narrative of normativity around Black death. In the silences of the gaps and vagaries that created the need for a social movement around #ArchivesForBlackLives, is the knowledge that tickets were sold to lynchings, that the mood of white mobs was exuberant – men cheering, women preening, children frolicking around the corpse as if it were a maypole ... [that] special excursion trains carried people to lynchings from farms and outlying areas, [and that] some lynchings were staged like theater, the victims dressed in costumes to deepen their degradation.[29]

Connecting permanence and oblivion to racial justice, Sutherland unites the current work of archivists with this troubled history of neglect. She asks: 'Why have American archives – through appraisal and other practices – extended amnesty to perpetrators of hate by refusing to document human rights abuses?'[30] David Greetham has written similarly on the 'cultural poetics of archival exclusion', and argues that we preserve that which is an idealised version of our achievements as people united, rather than memories of Auschwitz, Passchendaele, Hiroshima or My Lai.[31]

Following these claims from Sutherland and Greetham, I invite further exploration of how LIS professionals have conflated our collections with ourselves, or confused them with an idealised representation of ourselves. From the most horrifying histories of trauma on the scale of public lynchings or on the daily scale of microaggressions, can LIS professionals collect that which discomforts us? As Sutherland shows, librarians and archivists have chosen not to preserve white hate for fear of all that it represents or how it might contaminate. We're fearful of the symbolism of inclusion.[32]

---

28 Tonia Sutherland, 'Archival amnesty', pp. 1–22.

29 Ibid., p. 13.

30 Ibid., p. 2.

31 David Greetham, '"Who's in, who's out": the cultural poetics of archival exclusion', *Studies in the Literary Imagination*, 32 (1) (spring 1999): 9.

32 In contrast to the work of Caswell et al. on representational belonging in community archives, or larger works on community involvement in the construction of their own histories, here I am following Sutherland ('Archival amnesty') to suggest that institutional archives and permanent collections in libraries can include the work of racists without empowering such ideas or inviting racists to be part of the project of the archive or permanent collection; that they would not hold power over how their work is arranged and described. Michelle Caswell, Marika Cifor and Mario H. Ramirez, '"To suddenly discover yourself existing": uncovering

Inclusion in collections

In her book, *On Being Included: Racism and Diversity in Institutional Life*, Sara Ahmed discusses how institutions become instituted over time. She examines what we accept as 'second nature', 'how things are', or background, 'accumulated and sedimented history' or 'frozen history that surfaces as nature'.[33] She writes, 'Acts of naming, of giving buildings names, can keep a certain history alive: in the surroundings you are surrounded by who was there before. A history of whiteness can be a history of befores'.[34] In a recent talk, Ahmed used the example of a building at University College London still named for Francis Galton, a proponent of the eugenics movement. When pressed about continuing to uphold this legacy, the college's provost claimed his only defence to be that 'I inherited him'.[35] I argue here that LIS is still wrestling with our inheritances, not yet seeing them as alterable. Christine Pawley writes, 'Library collections themselves constitute a kind of legacy – one that successive generations of librarians inherit and tend to take for granted.'

Ahmed's larger project has been to examine and challenge discourses surrounding diversity work in institutions. Many important articles have been published recently critiquing diversity discourses in LIS. For example, David James Hudson critiqued the prevalent use of inclusion as the 'defining anti-racist modality within LIS', disagreeing with 'a simplistic equation of racism with exclusion':

> From the standpoint of the diversity literature, in other words, racism is a problem because it segregates, shuts out, or ignores nonwhite people and perspectives. Regimes of racial subordination are far more multifaceted in their operations, however, and, far from exclusion, have frequently taken the form of integration, whether through assimilation, cooptation, or more complex strategies of inclusive control...To limit LIS anti-racism to a politics of inclusion and diversification leaves little room for asking deeper questions about the ways in which more fundamental assumptions and structures within the library world operate as sites for the perpetuation of white supremacy — the reproduction of white normativity and citizenry through public library programming, for example; the extension of racialized colonial narratives of Western civilizational superiority through the development logics of LIS

the impact of community archives', *The American Archivist*, 79 (1) (1 Jun. 2016): 56–81. See https://doi.org/10.17723/0360-9081.79.1.56 (accessed 19 Jun. 2018).

33 Sara Ahmed, *On Being Included: Racism and Diversity in Institutional Life* (Durham, NC: Duke University Press, 2012).

34 Ibid., p. 38.

35 Ahmed, 'The institutional as the usual: diversity work as data collection'. Lecture, Barnard Center for Research on Women, New York, NY, 16 Oct. 2017.

global information inequality discourse; or the centering of a
putatively benevolent heteronormative white femininity as the
defining figure of North American library history.[36]

When we contemplate all of the work that is housed within libraries and
archives throughout America, we are certain to find a vast representation of
works made by, for and upholding whiteness. All too often when confronted
with the stranglehold of whiteness in our collections, librarians respond
by arguing for inclusion. A common solution introduced to address the
overpowering whiteness of our collections is to add work made by people of
colour (and, as Hudson also describes, this inclusion in collection development
often simultaneously functions as a reprieve from ensuring the hiring of
library workers of colour).[37] But how could current collecting displace all that
we have inherited? How can we believe that adding the works of people of
colour solves issues of racial injustice in our profession? Especially knowing
the barriers to publishing encountered by people of colour?[38]

Ahmed spoke about being willing to dismantle the university in order
to make it accommodate those who it was not originally built for (people
of colour, queer people, female-identified persons). As she put plainly, 'If
talking about sexism and racism damages institutions, we need to damage
institutions.'[39]

In two recent pieces, Hudson has discussed the distance from theory for
library and archives professionals, and has tied theoretical thinking to issues
surrounding race and white dominance in the profession.[40] He argues that the
profession remains undertheorised, but especially so in areas of broad social
phenomena, like race, whose 'historical operations are complex, constantly
shifting, and often contradictory where the methodologies upon which such
inquiry turns tend to be dismissed, implicitly or explicitly, as impractical.'[41]

Theory may be the thing that helps us damage our institutions, our
libraries, their collections.

36   David James Hudson, 'On "diversity" as anti-racism in library and information studies: a
      critique', *Journal of Critical Library and Information Studies*, 1 (1) (31 Jan. 2017), p. 13. See
      http://libraryjuicepress.com/journals/index.php/jclis/article/view/6 (accessed 19 Jun. 2018).
      ITE FOUND

37   Ibid.

38   See Jody Nyasha Warner, 'Moving beyond whiteness in North American academic libraries',
      Libri, 51 (3) (2001): 167–72. See www.researchgate.net/publication/266884155_Moving_
      Beyond_Whiteness_in_North_American_Academic_Libraries (accessed 19 Jun. 2018).

39   Ahmed, 'The institutional'.

40   Hudson, 'On diversity'. Also 'The whiteness of practicality', in Gina Schlesselman-Tarango (ed.)
      Topographies of Whiteness, pp. 203–34.

41   Hudson, 'On diversity', p. 26.

Conclusion

The time has come, God knows, for us to examine ourselves, but we can only do this if we are willing to free ourselves of the myth of America and try to find out what is really happening here.[42]

James Baldwin

Because race is a construct, how we classify and define racism is a process that continually shifts. Thinking about the historical documentation of racism at the WHS allowed me to 'lift the lid', as Ahmed instructs, and has been important to my development as a librarian.[43] Yet I don't know if the work I did with Danky can inherently be understood to be anti-racist or significantly contributes to the fight against white supremacy. Or, if these collections will shift in purpose as the larger WHS (and librarianship) ages and grows. Gathering together the work of white supremacists might seem the furthest way of working towards racial justice, but I do feel that this work connects to seeing beyond mythology and domination, and that it is linked to bearing witness.

Michelle Caswell recently spoke about how her scholarship aims to interrogate and dismantle white supremacy. She feels the need to confront this issue as a white person.[44] I feel the same need, and this chapter is an attempt to ask my white colleagues to examine their actions, and to face uncomfortable histories. I strongly recommend that LIS professionals continue to see even aged collections as sites for new theories and to frame our tragically white collections as opportunities for clear critique and re-examination. Though my argument here is that heinous materials must be preserved, I make it in order to confront whiteness in and outside of our profession and to stand alongside those who have been targeted by racial violence.

I wish to re-emphasise that I have been arguing for documenting white hate in our collections, not welcoming it into our communities. I do believe that we can make such distinctions.[45] Here my arguments for gathering together the work of white hate groups are know-your-enemy ones, not free speech debates. I am not concerned with the supposed neutrality of LIS, nor ('both sides') approaches to collecting where the left is balanced by the right – as if life could be so simple and binary. I am interested in discussing what happens to our work when we think of collections as potential sites of evidence, as ways of holding ourselves accountable, or lenses through which we might see structures of domination, beyond inclusion.

42 From 'The discovery of what it means to be an American', in *Nobody Knows My Name: More Notes of a Native Son* (New York, NY: Vintage Books, 1993), pp. 3–12 at p. 11.

43 Ahmed, 'The institutional'.

44 Michelle Caswell, 'Archivists against history repeating itself: towards a liberatory now'. Lecture, CUNY Graduate Center, New York, NY, 19 Oct. 2017.

45 Unlike a white librarian's recent social media post or statements put forth by the American Library Association, I am not suggesting that by collecting works of white hate groups we also perform outreach to them, allow them to meet in our public spaces, or allow members of the alt-right to speak at our universities.

Finally, I wish to wage a support campaign for healing justice.[46] Documenting white hate is not a project that one can endure full time, and my hope is that only so many institutions might engage in this work, enough to record these conversations adequately but not to glorify them.

Why should we preserve works of hate that are difficult to comprehend? Because it was in the air around us. These views were shared; this violence happened. We cannot ignore it.

46 See Patrice Cullor's discussion of healing justice in her interview, 'Ruby Sales: where does it hurt?', *On Being* project podcast audio, 17 Aug. 2017, https://onbeing.org/programs/ruby-sales-where-does-it-hurt-aug2017/ (accessed 19 Jun. 2018).

3. 'Mind meddling': exploring drugs and radical psychiatry in archives*

Lucas Richert

In 2015, *The Lancet* called for an end to bans on certain psychedelic drugs. The article lamented the loss of a superior understanding of the brain and better treatments for conditions such as depression and post-traumatic stress disorder (PTSD). It criticised the mental health treatment industry for failing to advance therapies beyond the golden era of the 1950s, and lambasted drug regulators for prohibiting psychedelic drugs, including LSD, ecstasy (MDMA) and psilocybin. These drugs had historically held clinical promise, but were 'designated as drugs of abuse' for various reasons.[1]

Lengthier pieces in *The New Yorker*, *The Atlantic* and other major periodicals soon followed on the *Lancet*'s heels. Together, they brought attention to a growing contention among researchers, and even some regulators, that a moral panic about drug abuse – rather than a more rational approach based on scientific evidence – stymied psychedelic drugs' clinical potential. As a result, the fields of psychiatry and psychology were lacking options for patients in the UK, US and beyond.

As a scholar ploughing medical history fields, this was quite a revelation to me. My research until then had centred on the American pharmaceutical industry – Big Pharma. And I had just signed a contract to write a new book called *Strange Trips: Science, Culture, and the Regulation of Drugs*, which was partially focused on researching the so-called love drug known as MDMA (aka 3,4-Methylenedioxymethamphetamine). That the mainstream press would give such attention to my topics – to LSD and ecstasy – was startling. I was only just starting to plan my archival research, write up my preliminary findings, and pursue some interviews. There was suddenly a lot more to consider.

* Thanks to Professor Erika Dyck, Professor Wendy Kline and the Staff Development Fund at Strathclyde University. I would also like to acknowledge the Radical Collections organisers particularly Jordan Landes and my co-panellists, Lisa Redlinski and Wendy Russell.

1 Ben Sessa, 'Turn on and tune in to evidence-based psychedelic research', *Lancet Psychiatry*, 2 (1) (2015): 10–12; James Randerson, 'Lancet calls for LSD in labs', *The Guardian*, 14 Apr. 2006. See www.theguardian. Com. /science/2006/apr/14/medicalresearch.drugs (accessed 19 Jun. 2018).

This chapter flows from these considerations and others arising from the excellent Radical Collections conference at the University of London in 2017. It will examine the above debates as well as explore the ways in which researchers, archivists and funders interact to create historical analyses, medical knowledge and policy. What role, I wonder, do funding bodies play in determining what is known about drugs and mental health? How does this, in turn, impact researchers in the lab *and* the library? What part does radicalism have to play in archives and beyond? I do not pretend to have satisfactory answers to these questions but in addressing them, I think that it facilitates a more complete picture of how medical knowledge has been established and codified, and certain medicines legitimised. More generally, it may be possible to develop a better view of the relationship between various parties, including researchers and archivists, funders and policymakers.

Historical background: psychedelic drugs and psychiatry in flux

Historians of medicine have long understood that drugs conform to cyclical careers or patterns involving intense periods of enthusiasm, therapeutic optimism, critical appraisals and eventually limited use.[2] Complex factors including biomedical research, marketing, industry and consumer demands have influenced these patterns. The length of time the cycles run for differs, but the overall model is a useful one for considering the lifecycle of a drug. Alternatives in medicine, in short, appear and disappear as mainstream selects, refines or rejects them; new alternatives are constantly generated by the limitations and weaknesses of the elite practices they run alongside.

In the realm of psychiatry, practices evolve as well. This might be called a pendulum swing. One needn't think any further than the erstwhile acceptance of leather restraints, penny viewings, lobotomy and hydrotherapy to see the swing in action. Not that long ago homosexuality was classified as a mental disorder. Now psychopharmacology, based on neuroscience and randomised controlled drug trials, serve as the dominant form of treatment in the mental health field.[3]

All of this is to suggest that the history of health and medicine demonstrates change over time. A push-and-pull between the insiders and outsiders – between professionals and quacks – has typified medical practice. Take insights from Collins's and Pinch's *Dr. Golem*, for example, which focus on the perennial tension between 'science and succor' or the struggle between well-regarded, evidence-based therapies and the psychic

2   See especially, Stephen Snelders, Charles Kaplan and Toine Peters, 'On cannabis, chloral hydrate, and career cycles of psychotropic drugs in medicine', *Bulletin for Medical History*, 80 (1) (2006): 95–114; David Musto, *Origins of Narcotic Control* (Oxford: Oxford University Press, 1999).

3   Lucas Richert and Frances Reilly, 'Book reviews: American psychiatry scholarship: the pendulum maintains its momentum', *Medical History*, 58 (4) (2014): 614–18.

needs of the patient. Certain psychedelics drugs blended with and reinforced alternative medicines and mental health treatments in California and beyond. These drugs, which form the basis of this discussion, underscore the line that separates consumer protection and product innovation, the public and the marketplace, the right to choose one's medicine and the state's obligation to protect citizens from spurious drugs.[4]

The period of the 1950s to the 1970s was one of great change and flux within the history of drugs and psychiatry. It was at times radical, and certainly contained a plethora of ideas and therapies. Anti-psychiatry, led by R.D. Laing, David Cooper, Joseph Berke and Leon Redler, for example, produced some of the earliest critiques of psychiatry. During 1967–8, a Radical Caucus was formed in the American Psychiatric Association and journals with such names as *The Radical Therapist* and *Issues in Radical Therapy* were published. 'Therapy means political change', the radical psychiatrists averred, not simply 'peanut butter'. These radicals were concerned about Vietnam, civil rights, feminism and lesbian, gay, bisexual and transgender issues, all of which fed into arguments about psychiatric service delivery and deinstitutionalisation.

Research: visiting collections

It became clear early on that collections and archives would determine the success of my project. Due to its broad nature, I opted to create a bibliography of secondary sources as well as identify archival sources in the United States, Canada and the United Kingdom. The diversity of the collections was also eye-opening. In the UK, I singled out and/or visited several archives, including:
- Dame Cicely Saunders Collection, King's College London
- R.D. Laing Collection, University of Glasgow
- Troubled Minds, King's College London
- Institute of Psychoanalysis
- Dingwall Collection, Senate House Library

What stood out most to me was that all these collections were funded through the Wellcome Trust's Research Resources Grants scheme aimed at 'improving access to health-related library and archive collections across the UK and Republic of Ireland by supporting cataloguing, conservation and digitisation projects.' This private trust funds researchers in the arts and the humanities at all career stages, promotes collaborations across research groups, and supports academic research centres.[5] As of this writing, I have consulted the Saunders papers and the Laing papers in Glasgow.

At the R.D. Laing Collection in my home city of Glasgow, archivists insisted on a thorough initial meeting about my project(s). In recent years, Laing has generated publicity, especially with the release of a film starring actor David

---

4   Harry Collins and Trevor Pinch, *Dr. Golem: how to Think About Medicine* (Chicago, IL: University of Chicago Press, 2005).

5   See https://wellcome.ac.uk/funding/research-resources-grants-support-libraries-and-archives (accessed 18 Jun. 2018).

Tennant. It came as no surprise, then, that keepers of the collection would be mindful and meticulous about who gained access to certain sensitive materials. Was I legitimate? Trustworthy? Would I do the source material justice? Indeed, the curators of the Laing Collection wished to review my slides before I delivered my lecture at the Radical Collections conference.

My experiences and thoughts about collections in North America were rather different. For example, public funding seemed more prevalent in Canada. A colleague of mine, Professor Erika Dyck, created an LSD database mostly funded by Canada's Social Sciences and Humanities Research Council (SSHRC). The project established an LSD archive based on Hollywood Hospital records (a clinic in Vancouver). The files – some patient files, others hospital records – offer an unprecedented opportunity to investigate the debate over how the use of psychedelic drugs in this context meddled with the mind. The collection presents a chance to move beyond 'generalized analyses, or policy imperatives, and instead to concentrate on the plight of addicts themselves and produce a more comprehensive picture of how addiction has been historically treated and conceptualized'.[6]

In addition, the History of Madness in Canada site was a useful resource. It is funded by Associated Medical Services Inc. (Toronto), SSHRC and Canadian Institutes of Health Research, as well as the University of Saskatchewan and Simon Fraser University. At the Provincial Archives of Saskatchewan, where I learned about hallucinogenic research in the 1950s, the archivists were just as meticulous but did not request a preliminary meeting to discuss the focus of my project. At the Centre for Addiction and Mental Health in Toronto, however, the corporate archivist was hands-on, and proved instrumental in my being able to secure rare documents and photographs.

What's left? My project continues to expand. As I mentioned at the Radical Collections conference, I needed to visit US archives. In particular, I will examine papers in the psychoactive substances research collections at the Virginia Kelly Karnes Archives and Special Collections Research Center, Purdue University. The collection was kickstarted in 2006 as a shared effort between Purdue pharmacology professor David Nichols, the Purdue University Libraries and the Betsy Gordon Foundation. Nichols, who retired from Purdue in 2012, was one of the country's leading experts on psychoactive drugs. The collection holds a range of materials that will be valuable, including manuscripts, research notes, correspondence, photographs and artefacts. In addition to the researchers' work, the archives also contain first-hand accounts from research participants.

6   See http://research-groups.usask.ca/history-medicine/research.php (accessed 18 Jun. 2018).

Conclusions

A few issues arose after I embarked on this project about radical psychiatry and medicines. Much historical and contemporary discussion about mental health and psychiatry has revolved around proper treatment models. Both scholars and the public at large have long been drawn to the various methods in which shrinks, employing everything from psychoanalysis to lobotomy and psychopharmacology, have attempted to address mental illness. Whether sponsored by government programmes or private initiatives, the creation of scientific/medical knowledge for mental illness has aroused a mixture of enthusiasm and criticism.

As the National Health Service is squeezed and more and more questions are asked about care provisions, scholars in the social sciences and humanities can contribute. Radical librarians, archivists and curators will also play a large role in this. If anything, as I've conducted my research it has become clear that stark differences exist in how data are stored and distributed. There are alternative ways of guarding the information, of interacting with the gatekeepers and of interpreting materials.

I've slowly got to grips with the fact that the collecting, archiving and issuing of materials can be radical acts. That is, in archives, radical politics and practices have tremendous impact on what I do – on what I can achieve as a researcher. Archives might be radical in form or function. They certainly trade in the 'past' and they might be active in the present. Thus, archives influence the future of scholarship. What I've learned, in short, is that radicalism (or lack thereof) shapes my views on drugs, medicine, health and so much more.

In the course of my research, I have also come to understand that archives can be developed in multiple ways. Around the world, new collections have been underwritten by a variety of sources. Collections are being developed for mass public consumption and with wider public engagement strategies in mind. This is certainly the case in the UK, supported by the Wellcome Trust. Collections and websites have been developed by researchers themselves and community partners. Here funding emanates from public and private sources. The question this immediately raises has to do with the accessibility of funding streams and the consumption of materials, for which I don't have a reasonable answer. Radical psychiatry and the use of drugs has a varied (largely untold) history. Such history, in turn, will influence science, medicine and public health. Archives and special collections, be they radical or not, will shape that history.

4. Cataloguing the radical material: an experience requiring a flexible approach

Julio Cazzasa

A wide-ranging number of collections, from manuscripts and early printing to twentieth-century rare materials and archives, are housed in Senate House Library's (SHL) Special Collections section. This chapter focuses on a proportion of this valuable material: in general, that which is related to radical (mostly reformist) movements from the nineteenth and twentieth centuries.[1] Although the materials cannot all be defined as radical, they do have a common theme in that they challenge the 'status quo' of their period in one way or another.

It is a challenge taking a more specific approach to cataloguing the material held in SHL's Special Collections. This is due to the variety of subjects and languages involved and to the need to deliver a comprehensive bibliographic record within a specific timeframe to make them available to readers. At the same time this is the beauty of working with these collections. At the outset, it is not always possible to form an exact idea of what will emerge from one's work with a new collection and this can also be true even when the cataloguing is almost complete. Every item needs careful scrutiny. At times, when searching databases for a record to work with, it is not uncommon for negative results to come up, meaning that EMMA records[2] must then be produced.

Another point is the current trend for all such collections to be digitised. Aside from the need to check copyrights and other potential issues (legal and practical), what is clear is that they need to be catalogued accurately, whether digitised or not. The objective is to have all the material catalogued and accessible to researchers and readers (via the online catalogue).

Preserving these collections is essential if we are to understand the past and the present, and even more so when society is undergoing deep change. It is our task, as cataloguers, to make them available to scholars to help them find answers to important contemporary questions.

---

1   For more see Senate House Library's Radical Voices exhibition website at www. senatehouselibrary.ac.uk/exhibitions-and-events/exhibitions/radical-voices (accessed 20 Jun. 2018). I have also referred throughout to the *Oxford Dictionary of National Biography* at www.oxforddnb.com (accessed 20 Jun. 2018).
2   Records done from scratch.

The collections mentioned here are varied in nature. Some focus on a single subject such as the Pelling collection (history of the Labour Party), whereas others cover a range of subjects (for example, the Heisler collection with its left-wing literature in various languages from diverse geo-locations, and a few additional surprises). The third is the Latin American political pamphlets collection which contains material from a variety of sources mainly from the decades of conflict, the 1960s, 1970s and 1980s, covering all countries in this region. The material is written in Spanish as well as languages such as Portuguese, English, French and Italian.

Ron Heisler collection

Ron Heisler, a book collector, trade unionist and socialist started to collect political literature at the age of eighteen, and began to donate it to SHL in 2004. He regards the library as the ideal place to preserve his material and is eager to continue adding more new titles to the catalogue on a regular basis.

The collection currently comprises approximately 25,000 books, 20,000 pamphlets, 3,000 journal and newspaper titles from the eighteenth to the twentieth century and a quantity of ephemera, published by or relating to labour and radical political movements, and to political expression in art, drama and literature. There is a particular emphasis on Britain and Ireland including items published by radical groups, friendly societies and the Chartists from the late eighteenth to the twentieth century, and many publications from Trotskyist groups, the Independent Labour Party and the Communist Party from the early to mid twentieth century. In terms of local and desktop publishing, British material dating from the 1960s is particularly strong. The holdings of New Left material from the 1960s and 1970s are very extensive, and there are some quite rare publications which emerged from the women's movement.

Included in the collection are a number of rare titles which – together with the ephemera printed in flyers and pamphlets (usually produced to promote political rallies) – are unique for many reasons, potentially because they were banned, or produced in small quantities. As a result, these are scarce and a relatively high proportion of original cataloguing has been necessary, that is, describing material from scratch, as opposed to being able to download and adapt a catalogue record from another UK or US research library or the OCLC network.[3] In this way, the cataloguer of these documents gains a real sense of contributing to research and providing access to a distinctive collection. It can be said that when a new title from the Heisler collection is catalogued, the chances of it being requested shortly afterwards are high because this collection is already well known and used by academics and students.

---

3   A global library cooperative supporting thousands of libraries in making information more accessible and useful to people around the world.

For this chapter I have selected examples related to the first Spanish Civil War, '19 de Julio 1936: España' (Heisler P2248). This is a propaganda print published in Barcelona by the Confederación Nacional del Trabajo (CNT, National Confederation of Labour) y la Federación Anarquista Ibérica (Iberian Anarchist Federation) umbrella organisation to which the CNT belonged. The 'avant garde' design and the quality of the print is eye-catching, no less the contents (about the defeat of the fascists in their first attempt to dominate Catalonia). Notable in this propaganda is the presence of women filling roles usually reserved for men in what was an extremely patriarchal society.

On the same theme the next example, the 'International Brigade British battalion: national memorial meeting' (Heisler P2786) refers to Brigade members' arrival back in the country after the Republican government had sent them back before Catalonia fell. A crowd of about 7,000 met them at Victoria station on December 1937.[4] This memorial programme was organised to recognise their fight against fascism and pay tribute to the fallen comrades.

Cataloguing this multilingual collection of wide-ranging subjects from all over the world – with the over-arching subject of left-wing

Heisler P2248

literature – as well as handling an extensive number of titles, has been a real challenge. Unusually, we also had the advantage of regular personal contact with the donor (an SHL reader) who frequently checked on progress via the public online catalogue. This could have been a disadvantage but was quite the

---

4   Tom Buchanan, 'The impact of the Spanish Civil War on Britain: war loss and memory' (Brighton: Sussex Academic Press, 2007).

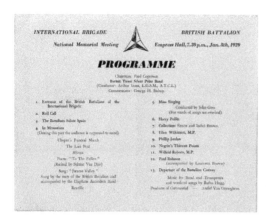

opposite. We benefited from his input whenever he visited our office. This included the stories behind some of the material particularly people mentioned in the literature and the ownership signatures, a regular feature. Each crate I open is always the start of a fascinating journey of discovery. But most of all I have to resist the temptation to stop and read entire publications whenever an interesting theme piques my curiosity.

Heisler P2786

Pelling collection

The collector Henry Mathison Pelling (1920–97) was a historian best known for his works on the history of the British Labour Party. When he died the collection went to Professor Alastair Reid (himself a trade union and labour historian at Cambridge) who donated it to SHL.

The collection comprises some 800 British left-wing political pamphlets from the 1880s to the 1970s. Many emanate from or pertain to the Communist Party of Great Britain. Others concern the Labour Party, the Independent Labour Party and the Red International of Labour Unions, with a few anti-Communist pamphlets. Items range from leaflets and newsletters to substantial booklets and cover such topics as election manifestos, conference reports, lectures, party manuals, histories and song books. The material on the World War II period is comprehensive. Records are not available in OCLC or CURL[5] for some ten per cent of the total, meaning that this particular

---

5   An abbreviation for 'Client URL Request Library'. Its aim is to increase the ability of research libraries to share resources among themselves. The holdings of these libraries provide the basis of the Copac online catalogue.

material is very likely to be unique. In addition, the rest of the collection is not widely available and, of course, is not gathered together in one place.

The examples selected here relate to the Spanish Civil War. 'Back from the dead; by Jack Coward, with a foreword by Harry Pollitt (Pelling 23 (17)), is the personal narrative of an International Brigade member. The civil war also forms part of 'It can be done: report of the Fourteenth Congress of the Communist Party of Great Britain, Battersea, May 29–31, 1937' (Pelling 20 (08)) and includes a Roll of Honour. Finally, an anonymous story, 'In Spain with the International Brigade: a personal narrative' (Pelling 31 (11)) is an interesting example of war propaganda. Its author is an unidentified English working man who served in the International Brigade, became disillusioned and tried to discourage others from joining the struggle. It is noteworthy that the publisher, Burns Oates & Washbourne, is an English Catholic publishing house which at the time was the Holy See's official publisher in England.

To a certain extent cataloguing this material was complementary to the work I was already doing on the Heisler collection among others. Although only a small collection, it was full of surprises. Nearly ten per cent of the records had to be created from scratch. The material was quite unique and in ensuring that all relevant information was captured and subject headings were both accurate and appropriate, careful attention to detail was called for. In

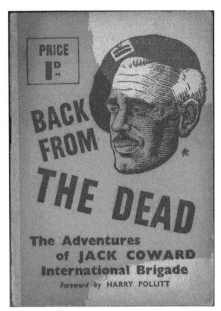

Pelling 23 (17)

Pelling 20 (08)

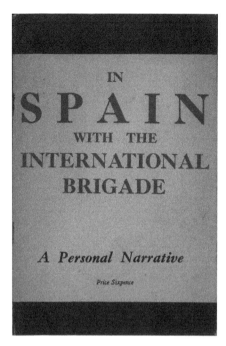

my case it was most enlightening to learn about the development of different expressions of left-wing politics in Britain as well as the development of the Labour Party during the twentieth century.

Pelling 31 (11)

Latin American political pamphlets collection

When the Contemporary Archive on Latin America closed in 1986, its holdings were donated to the Institute of Latin American Studies, thus forming the basis of its Latin American political pamphlets collection. With subsequent additions it now comprises some 140 boxes of pamphlets, posters, reports, miscellaneous journals and other ephemera, produced by political parties, pressure groups and non-governmental organisations (NGOs), trade unions and governments. The materials are written predominantly in Spanish and Portuguese, though a significant proportion of them are in English as well as other languages such as Italian and French.

A violent chapter in the history of Latin America is revealed in the documents that can be found in the section devoted to 1960–80. Indeed, for some, the roots of this violence can be traced as far back as the beginning of the twentieth century, mainly in the form of state repression in which security forces played a central role.

Importantly, the ephemera in the collection were originally processed as part of a project that included similar material from Commonwealth countries. The collection is distinctive in that the items have been catalogued not as part of an archive but as printed material. This means that although each pamphlet has a bibliographical record, the classmarks have been organised by box, making the retrieval of particular items difficult and time-consuming and sometimes leading to material being misplaced. For this reason, a project to improve the management of the collection was set up between 2014 and 2015 with the help of multilingual volunteers. It culminated in a seminar for scholars, researchers and anyone else with a special interest in the subject to promote their use of these documents.

Every country in the region is represented, but I will mention just a couple of examples here. First, the Chilean material covering the build-up to and the aftermath of the 1973 coup, including election posters and pamphlets written by apologists for the Pinochet regime. Second, prints from Bolivia, largely dating from the late 1970s and early 1980s including many rare or singular publications by the Partido Obrero Revolucionario (Revolutionary Workers Party), one of the only Trotskyist parties in history to garner a mass following.

The items I have selected are 'Cuba en Punta del Este' by Ernesto Che Guevara (EC 320 PAM/2/10) published in Caracas, Venezuela, which reproduces the original text from the Cuban newspaper *Prensa Libre*. It outlines the position put forward by Cuba at a summit of American states held in the Uruguayan resort. Another Cuban example but on a different subject is 'Meeting on the status of Latin-American and Caribbean women: speech June 7, 1985' by Fidel Castro (EC 320 PAM/2/04). I also include these three examples from Chile: 1) 'Cile' by the Comitato Vietnam (M 320 PAM/5/34), a pamphlet published circa 1974; 2) 'The

EC 320 PAM/2/10

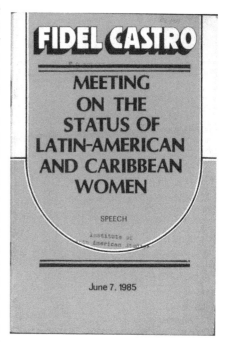

EC 320 PAM/2/04

M 320 PAM/5/34

Chilean government's declaration of principle' by Augusto Pinochet Ugarte, Jose T. Merino Castro, Cesar Mendoza Duran and Gustavo Leigh Guzman (M 320 PAM/5/39), a six-page pamphlet; and 3) 'Bautista Van Schowen: three years of torture and resistance' (M 320 PAM/5/23), published by the Movimiento de Izquierda Revolucionaria in 1976.

I aim with these few examples related mainly to two Latin American countries to give just a hint of what one can find in those boxes. Coming from a variety of sources, the materials cover a wide range of issues, making this a particularly valuable collection for those interested in researching this particular period of Latin America modern history.

M 320 PAM/5/39

M 320 PAM/5/23

The library has a real hidden treasure in this multilingual collection. Its contents are from a specific region and date from a more recent period than the other two collections. The cataloguing project described above got the collection off to a good start but thereafter it suffered a more complex history until transferred to the care of the Special Collections section. Much of the contents were identified only by boxes. Furthermore, because those who had previously worked on the collection did not have specialist knowledge, some items went missing or were temporarily misplaced. Key to the success of the project were the services of two student volunteers (both studying subjects related to Latin America), who helped to recover, order and give an individual classmark to approximately 4,000 items.

The most interesting part of the work involved examining individual items to check for any misspellings or anomalies within each record. This initial process paved the way for my work in sorting the items and if they had not been classified adding the correct cataloguing procedures to them. This allowed us to delve deep into the collection and discuss the subject matter as part of the work, giving the students a fresh, and sometimes different point of view to the bibliography available.

These three collections demonstrate that its holding of left-wing political literature forms an important hub within SHL's Special Collections wing. However, it is important to mention that there are other significant sections including the library of the labour leader and liberal minister, John Elliott Burns (1858–1943) and that of the Trotskyist historian and activist, Al Richardson (1941–2003). It is also worth adding that it is possible to discover a wealth of information in archival material from similar collections to that of Heisler. Material is also dispersed through other collections (for example, the Family Welfare Association) that are not specifically dedicated to political themes. In SHL therefore, the researcher could find, all in one place, a rich and extensive holding of distinctive and rare material complemented by its other research collections.

5. Decentring qualification: a radical examination of archival employment possibilities

Hannah Henthorn and Kirsty Fife

As two archive workers from marginalised backgrounds who have accessed MA courses through diversity schemes and scholarships, we wanted to produce a paper for the Radical Collections conference held on 3 March 2017 which would critically examine the current climate for archival employment and qualification, propose forward measures for change and suggest practical steps that can be taken to create more access routes into the profession. This chapter is an adapted version of that paper. We were responding to a recent National Archives (TNA) consultation paper on a new strategic vision for archives.[1] Later developed and published as *Archives Unlocked*,[2] it defined a 'diverse, flexible and skilled workforce' as an emerging priority for the archive sector's future development.

In the current climate where diversity and inclusion are becoming more present in our collecting, engagement and access agendas, those employed in the sector are all aware that work must be done to ensure that the individuals and community groups we wish to engage with are reflected in our workforce. However, the current processes for qualifying as an archivist actively exclude many marginalised people. With tuition fees increasing, apprenticeships paying inadequate wages, and scholarships and bursaries dwindling, the cost(s) of qualification are often too much for aspiring archivists to afford.

To give some background information about us, Kirsty Fife is curator of library and archives at the National Science and Media Museum in Bradford. She qualified as an archivist in 2013 after studying at University College London (UCL). She is a working-class queer disabled woman and accessed the archive profession through scholarship funding at UCL. Hannah Henthorn is currently studying archives and records management, as a distance-learning student, at the University of Dundee. She volunteers at the Royal College of Surgeons of Edinburgh, and has worked or volunteered at the National Records of

---

1   TNA, 'Consultation on a new strategic vision for the archive sector' (2016). See http://webarchive.nationalarchives.gov.uk/+/www.nationalarchives.gov.uk/documents/archives/consultation-strategic-vision-for-archives.pdf (accessed 25 Sep. 2017).

2   TNA, 'Archives unlocked'. See www.nationalarchives.gov.uk/archives-sector/projects-and-programmes/strategic-vision-for-archives/ (accessed 25 Sep. 2017).

Scotland and the Aberdeen City and Aberdeenshire Archives. She is a queer disabled woman, and was only able to access her diploma programme by means of a TNA bursary. It is important to acknowledge that we are white and British and recognise that other groups experience marginalisation in a way we do not. We do not speak on their behalf, but have prioritised the voices of people of colour in reviewing existing scholarship.

This chapter begins with a discussion of contemporary research regarding diversity and inclusion – both external to and within the archive profession. It then highlights some examples of existing diversity schemes run by organisations in this sector. Our own experiences of qualification are then described, and the chapter concludes with proposals for some forward steps for the sector to consider, both as professionals and as institutions.

In her book, *Living a Feminist Life*, Sara Ahmed refers to 'diversity work in two related senses: first, diversity work in the work we do when we are attempting to transform an institution; and second, diversity work is the work we do when we do not quite inhabit the norms of an institution.'[3] Our own impression that we do not, to borrow from Ahmed, 'inhabit the norms' of archive institutions has led us to begin this project together, writing from the position of two employees who work and study within these institutions, but who simultaneously have felt unwelcome and underconfident in our workplaces and study environments. We hope this chapter and our subsequent research together will encourage our colleagues and peers to interrogate the archive sector and the process of qualification as an archivist, as part of active work to diversify our collections and workplaces, and to consider the ways in which the current system can marginalise and exclude many groups, and the practical steps that the sector and we as professionals can take to create more access routes into this career.

Review of the literature

Existing literature, policies and schemes about diversity and inclusion in the archive workforce, both in the UK and internationally, will be explored in this section including reports and schemes by the Archives and Records Association (ARA), TNA, Society of American Archivists (SAA), and UCL. The academic research we draw on includes some of the broader pool of diversity research relating to employment in universities and other equivalent sectors.

Before examining the archive sector's approach to the need for diversity and inclusion, it must be understood that research in this area can, even unintentionally, ultimately be interdisciplinary – that is, the arguments in favour of diversity initiatives and inclusivity practices being applied across multiple sectors. A number of multidisciplinary and collaborative opportunities have taken place, from the one-day conference Making

---

3   Sara Ahmed, *Living a Feminist Life* (Durham, NC and London: Duke University Press, 2017), p. 91.

Diversity Research Everyone's Business, at the University of Birmingham on 22 September 2017,[4] to the establishment of fora such as the Essex Critical Diversity Research Group.[5] These have brought together academics and sector professionals to examine existing policy and legislation, while sharing insight into recent research and considering the challenges faced by policymakers and marginalised groups: those who would benefit the most from diversity policy and practice. Some of the most fundamental scholarship examining these issues comes from Sara Ahmed. Her *Living a Feminist Life* focuses on diversity policy and practice within universities and academia, and has many clear parallels with the work being started in this chapter, a relationship that will be explored below. Other key research can be found in Reynolds et al.,[6] who examined the barriers to career progression faced by disabled persons – interestingly, they do not just refer to denial of physical access (to buildings, for example), but denial of access to specific training and preparation for work, and exclusion based on job-design. Additionally, they note that disabled people are 'unjustly assessed' by a 'narrow and misplaced' definition of 'skill'.[7] The importance of addressing the lack of inclusivity in even the path towards the desired career is echoed by Kirton and Greene:[8]

> We start from the position that certain groups of people enter employment and organizations already disadvantaged by wider social inequalities as reflected in, for example, the education system. The discrimination they meet in employment reinforces their disadvantaged position and militates against their career progress.

In 2006, Kersley et al., based on their analysis of the results of the Workplace Employment Relations Survey (2004), recommended that minority groups 'underrepresented in the labour market' could be more encouraged to apply for vacant posts if they were actively targeted in recruitment – for example, with roles advertised in a variety of ethnic minority media, or simply by adding the statement in job listings that applications are 'explicitly welcome' from marginalised groups.[9]

4   University of Birmingham, Making Diversity Research Everyone's Business (2017). See www. birmingham.ac.uk/schools/business/research/creme/events/2017/09/Making-Diversity-Research-Everyones-Business.aspx (accessed 27 Oct. 2017).

5   University of Essex, Essex Business School, Essex Critical Diversity Research Group (2017). See https://www1.essex.ac.uk/ebs/research/diversity/default.aspx (accessed 27 Oct. 2017).

6   Gillian Reynolds, Phillip Nicholls and Caterina Alferoff, 'Disabled people, (re) training, and employment: a qualitative exploration of exclusion', in Mike Noon and Emmanuel Ogbonna (eds.) *Equality, Diversity and Disadvantage in Employment* (London: Palgrave Macmillan, 2001).

7   Ibid., p. 192.

8   Gill Kirton and Anne-Marie Greene, *The Dynamics of Managing Diversity: a Critical Approach* (London: Routledge, 2016), p. 6.

9   Barbara Kersley, Carmen Alpin, John Forth, Alex Bryson, Helen Bewley, Gill Dix and Sarah Oxenbridge, *Inside the Workplace: Findings from the 2004 Workplace Employment Relations Survey* (London: Routledge, 2004), p. 75.

Specific to the archives sector, the ARA has done periodic reports and research into analysing the makeup of the workforce in the UK. Most recently, a study of the UK information workforce, co-produced with the Chartered Institute of Library and Information Professionals (CILIP),[10] aimed to map the UK information workforce and identify key issues affecting those in the sector. The full results have yet to be published but the executive summary indicates a number of issues and notable points including:

- Men earning more than women, and a lack of women in leadership roles despite women otherwise far outnumbering men in the archive sector
- A larger proportion of the archive workforce are white than across other sectors (96.7 per cent compared with 85.7 per cent in the whole UK workforce)
- A smaller proportion of people with disabilities employed in the sector – 15.9 per cent with long-term health issues (compared to 18.1 per cent in the UK workforce).

The ARA-CILIP report does not survey certain areas of the workforce – for instance, there is nothing about anyone with gender identities other than male or female, and no data about sexuality. This lack makes it harder to draw conclusions about gender and sexual diversity in the archive sector, and can be raised as a diversity issue in itself. However, the demographics that have been reported on indicate a substantial lack of diversity in this workforce overall, consistency which means one could assume that it is also the case with unrepresented groups as well.

The archive sector's recent and historical academic research and policy documents do acknowledge the lack of diversity in the workforce as an issue. In late 2016 and early 2017, TNA began consulting about a new vision for the profession. A 'diverse, flexible and skilled workforce'[11] was defined as an emerging priority for the sector's future development. But this isn't an 'emerging' priority – the issue has been raised repeatedly for decades in various contexts. Seven years ago, TNA itself proposed an action plan to address their equality and diversity commitments, including developing internal internship guidance and using diversity networks within the media to advertise traineeships.[12]

Even earlier, in the late 1970s and early 1980s, the SAA, together with the American Association for State and Local History and the American Association/

10   ARA and CILP, 'A study of the UK information workforce'. See https://archive.cilip.org.uk/sites/default/files/documents/executive_summary_nov_2015-5_a4web.pdf (accessed 25 Sep. 2017).

11   NA, 'Consultation on a new strategic vision for the archive sector' (2016). See http://webarchive.nationalarchives.gov.uk/+/www.nationalarchives.gov.uk/documents/archives/consultation-strategic-vision-for-archives.pdf (accessed 25 Sep. 2017).

12   NA, 'Equality and diversity action plan April 2010–January 2012' (2012). See www.nationalarchives.gov.uk/documents/ed-action-plan-january-2012.xls (accessed 27 Oct. 2017).

Alliance of Museums, formed a joint committee to address the problems of minimal minority recruitment.[13] Alongside this was the establishment in 1987 of – what is now known as – the Archivists and Archives of Color Roundtable (AACR), which aims to 'identify and address' concerns facing minorities within the profession[14] (joined, later, by the Native American Archives Roundtable in 2005[15], and the Latin American and Caribbean Cultural Heritage Archives Roundtable in 2008).[16] The SAA have established various scholarships in recent years to support students from minority backgrounds.[17]

In 1996 Kathryn M. Neal circulated a survey to archivists of colour in the United States, the results of which were published in her article 'The importance of being diverse: the archival profession and minority recruitment'. Neal sees the benefits of having more archivists of colour working in the sector as including improving 'donor relations (for instance, how to approach and document members of growing communities of color most effectively)' and 'reference/access (determining how to improve services as user groups become increasingly diverse, or how to attract a more diverse pool of researchers if society's changing demographics are not reflected).'[18] The survey, answered by thirty archivists of colour based in the US, explored career experiences including entry into the profession, career progression and what they have encountered in their work in the archive sector. The article proposed several structural reasons for people of colour not commonly becoming archivists including the public image of the profession, the information sector's neglect of communities of colour, low graduation rates and economics. Neal's respondents proposed a number of steps to broaden the profession, including scholarships, mentoring programmes, working in partnership with university courses (particularly non-traditional), speaking to schools to introduce archives as a career at an earlier age, establishment of networks for people of colour in the profession, and internships targeted at people of colour with associated funding.

In the UK, a number of schemes have been introduced to provide new entry routes into the sector. Between 2005 and 2008, the University College London and TNA ran a joint diversity internship scheme, combining a year of study with a year of work – an opportunity created specifically to help ethnic

---

13   Kathryn M. Neal, 'The importance of being diverse: minority recruitment and the archival profession', *Archival Issues*, 21 (2) (1996): 145–58 at 147.

14   SAA, 'Archivists and Archives of Color Roundtable, 2012 Membership Directory'. See https://www2.archivists.org/sites/all/files/2012%20AAC%20Directory.pdf (accessed 29 Oct. 2017), p. 2.

15   SAA, 'Native American Archives section'. See https://www2.archivists.org/groups/native-american-archives-section (accessed 26 Oct. 2017).

16   SAA, 'Latin American and Caribbean Cultural Heritage Archives (LACCHA) section'. See https://www2.archivists.org/groups/latin-american-and-caribbean-cultural-heritage-archives-laccha-section (accessed 26 Oct. 2017).

17   SAA, 'Mosaic scholarship'. See https://www2.archivists.org/governance/handbook/section12-mosaic (accessed 30 Oct. 2017).

18   Neal, 'The importance of being diverse', p. 146.

minority students enter the profession.[19] More recently, TNA, in partnership with other archive organisations, has delivered Opening Up Archives and Transforming Archives traineeships. According to the TNA website,[20] the Transforming Archives programme aims to:

- Diversify the archives workforce
- Address gaps in the skills available in the archives workforce
- Provide new routes into working in the sector

A successful example of an Opening Up Archives traineeship was hosted by Tower Hamlets Local History Library and Archives.[21] This traineeship engaged with the Bengali community in Tower Hamlets, who were underrepresented in collections and as users but constituted 36 per cent of the local population. As the case study states, it was particularly important for stakeholders in the community to be heavily involved in the traineeships in terms of the person recruited, the recruiting panel, mentoring roles throughout the placement, and all project outputs. The description of the role explicitly cited relevant knowledge and cultural experience as essential. As well as benefiting the project, this also 'ensured that applicants with a Bengali background could compete on a level playing field with the many applicants seeking paid work in archives who may typically have had a more extensive or traditional work experience background.'[22] By valuing cultural knowledge and background as much as other more traditional archival skill sets, the traineeship actively made the space for a person from a different cultural background (that is, in this example, someone who came from a Bengali background as opposed to a white person) to take up the post. This benefited both the organisation and collections (via the acquisitions the traineeship facilitated) and also the sector more widely by creating a route into it for more diverse applicants. Conditions like these don't seem to have been widely applied across all traineeships hosted under this scheme, and would benefit from being embedded into the structure of a diversity programme from the beginning.

Between 2013 and 2016, TNA funded a series of diversity education bursaries.[23] For each year in this period, the institution issued two bursaries designed to 'support candidates in gaining a qualification by providing financial support and helping to address the socioeconomic barrier that exists for some who are considering entering into the archives sector.'[24] Preference

---

19 The Archival Education and Research Institute (AERI) and Pluralizing the Archival Curriculum Group (PACG), 'Education for the archival multiverse', *The American Archivist*, 74 (1) (2011): 69–101 at 74.

20 See www.nationalarchives.gov.uk/archives-sector/projects-and-programmes/transforming-archives/ (accessed 25 Sep. 2017).

21 NA, 'Opening up archives: Tower Hamlets Archives and Local History Library' (2011). See www.nationalarchives.gov.uk/archives-sector/case-studies-and-research-reports/case-studies/workforce-development/tower-hamlets/ (accessed 25 Sep. 2017).

22 Ibid.

23 'The National Archives diversity education bursary' (2013). See www.nationalmuseums.org.uk/media/job-pdfs/job-3309.pdf (accessed 5 Oct. 2017).

24 Ibid.

was given to applicants who identified as BAME (black and minority ethnic) and/or disabled. These bursaries were awarded up to £10,000 and were available to applicants undertaking full-time study in archives and records management, information management or humanities computing courses. Whereas the bursaries were a positive step for the sector, the limiting terms (full-time courses only) and the lack of a maintenance grant discriminated against those unable to do full-time study (including disabled archive workers) or those without socioeconomic support.

As illustrated above, a number of small schemes have aimed to tackle the lack of diversity in the archive sector. However, they often have stipulations and conditions that can actively exclude the groups they are aiming to encourage. Issues with traineeships can include wages which are less than living wage salaries, short-term contracts, no forward career progression or commitment to supporting postgraduate fees or study after completion of a contract. Scholarships are often only available on a full-time basis or only cover fees, which makes them accessible to a much smaller subset of applicants than those with more flexible conditions. Awards and schemes that aim to diversify the workforce but exclude their target applicants through imposing conditions do not challenge the sector, but do make archive institutions appear as if they are taking positive action. Sara Ahmed refers to this process and diversity in institutions more widely as 'a technique for rearranging things so organisations can appear in a better or happier way … Diversity is a way of rearranging a series that does not disrupt that series. This is why it is possible to talk about an image of diversity and everyone knows what you are referring to.'[25]

In her book, *Living a Feminist Life*, Ahmed explores this gap between words and action, and within the context of higher education and academia, writes about the idea of policy documentation as essentially meaningless unless accompanied by action:

> The university gets judged as good because of this [policy] document. It is this very judgment about the document that blocks action, producing a kind of 'marshmallow feeling', a feeling that we are doing enough, or doing well enough, or even that there is nothing left to do … writing policies becomes a substitute for action.[26]

The role of diversity work in this context is to connect words and action. Those employed in this area thus 'live in this gap between words and deeds, trying to make organizations catch up with the words they send out.'[27] The archive sector has policies that support diversity and limited opportunities and initiatives to facilitate change, but often those opportunities themselves are exclusive to those without privilege and support networks. In order to truly

25 Ahmed, *Living a Feminist Life*, p. 98.
26 Ibid., p. 104.
27 Ibid., p. 107.

diversify the sector, the profession as a whole needs momentum to effect structural change led jointly by sector bodies and marginalised workers, not sporadic and ill-funded opportunities.

More work needs to be done to analyse where these schemes have succeeded and where they have not, and in particular on the background and later career progression of participants. In 2012, Rabia Gibbs, who – before her death – served on the SAA's diversity committee and the AACR, examined the developmental history of African American archives, and questioned how we as a profession might make our diversity 'initiatives' more 'authentic and meaningful'. She asked, 'whose diversity agenda are we following – our profession's or ethnic communities' self-determined criteria?', imploring us to avoid a narrowing of diversity objectives.[28] It is important for us to critically analyse the work that happens in our sector, to continually ask ourselves whether our policies and schemes are affecting positive change.

Case studies

The following two case studies illustrate our own experiences of qualification as archivists and archive sector workers. Both of us accessed funding towards our postgraduate studies by means of diversity schemes and scholarships run by universities, and from the basis of our experiences in the profession, we wish to use this platform to speak candidly about what we have encountered when navigating access to funding and qualification as two marginalised people. Hannah's case study explores what she had to contend with when accessing a diversity education bursary from TNA, and Kirsty's explores her experience of scholarship funding at UCL. The precariousness of scholarship and bursary funding in the current financial climate means that often schemes exist in the short term, so it is impossible to monitor their successes and failures over a longer term. We hope these case studies will help to contribute the lived experiences of accessing these schemes to scholarship and reports on diversity schemes and funding opportunities, and the development of future similar schemes and funding.

1: Hannah's diversity education bursary from TNA

At present I'm a distance-learning student at the University of Dundee, on the archives and records management programme. I've been volunteering and working at a number of heritage organisations since late 2011, while studying at the University of Aberdeen. I realised after starting my MLitt in early modern studies that I wanted to be an archivist, and I resolved to get whatever practical experience I could before applying for the Dundee diploma. My postgraduate degree actually had to be done part-time – I couldn't afford the full-time fees upfront, and I still needed to work multiple

28   Rabia Gibbs, 'The heart of the matter: the developmental history of African American archives', *The American Archivist*, 75 (1) (2012): 195–204 at 199.

jobs to pay my rent, my living costs, and my tuition. Finding jobs in the archives sector that could fit around my studies and my shift patterns, while also providing me with the professional experience required for the Dundee application, meant that I spent the majority of my master's juggling three jobs and two volunteering roles. I also have an autoimmune disease and a chronic pain condition, with varying severity of symptoms – when I first started to seriously consider a career in archives, I was often relying on the care of my partner, the use of walking aids, and would sometimes be housebound with fatigue or joint pain.

This was in fact the primary reason for wanting to get my archives qualification with the University of Dundee. Their distance-learning course meant that I could stay wherever my partner was based, have my care needs met, and not have such a conflicting schedule of work, classes and health management. Faced with the fact that I could barely afford my master's programme and my living costs in Aberdeen, not to mention coping with a disability that could threaten any semblance of financial stability, my archives diploma seemed like a pipe dream. It was either going to be something that I could never afford, or would have to spend several years saving up for. With everything I had learned about archiving through my volunteering roles, I wanted to know more, I wanted to understand more, and I needed to channel this passion into getting the qualification that would open more doors into the sector.

In January 2015, I discovered that TNA ran a diversity education bursary scheme – at the time, this afforded a funding opportunity for two new students from under-represented groups (with a particular focus on BAME and disabled applicants). However, having applied for the distance-learning programme at the University of Dundee, which takes between two-and-a-half and five years to complete, I was unable to meet the criteria of a one-year, full-time qualification. But I asked TNA if I could apply anyway, believing that it was most unlikely I would get anywhere – I argued that the distance-learning course would give me the opportunity to enter my dream profession, while recognising how my health required an alternative study model. And, given that the bursary board were keen for applications from disabled applicants, widening the scope of its criteria would acknowledge the kinds of flexibility we may need due to our disabilities, and be a positive step for disabled access into the sector.

2: Kirsty's qualification via Arts and Humanities Research Council (AHRC) studentship

In 2015 I wrote a blog post called 'The cost(s) of being an archivist'[29] which explored socioeconomic barriers to working in the archive sector. The piece was written from my own perspective, as a working-class woman, two years after I qualified as an archivist. To give some background to my career history,

29   In *The Museum Blog Book* (Museums Etc: Edinburgh and Boston, 2017).

I started as a digitisation officer for photography and film collections after studying photographic arts for my undergraduate degree. Initially, as a photographer, this was a logical job for me to take on but over the two years I spent working in this field I became much more interested in cataloguing, interpretation and access, and decided that I wanted to qualify as an archivist. As I come from a working-class background, I was unable to access any financial support towards my MA and had to pursue alternative routes to pay for my postgraduate qualification.

In the blog post and essay I created the following list of expenses, covering the cost of my education, periods of unemployment between contracts, and of moving across the country to take up new roles. I was interested in mapping out the financial commitment and opportunity cost required to access a professional role in the sector. The breakdown was as follows:

- 2005–8: Undergraduate degree, c.£24,000
- 2009–10: First entry-level job in archives, which paid £1k less than national minimum wage
- 2010–11: Cross-country move to take up a contract post, £1,500
- 2012: Cross-country move to start MA at UCL, £2,000
- 2012–13: MA qualification, c.£20,000 (funded by AHRC scholarship, fees + maintenance)
- 2009–14: Periods of no work due to contracts finishing, c.£6,400 (estimate based on equivalent benefits)

That's a total of £54,900. This was without having had to volunteer, unlike many of my peers, a factor that would undoubtedly push the total up significantly. Anyone qualifying now would pay substantially more in undergraduate fees as well, which were £1,100 when I went to university in 2005.

A UCL scholarship funded me through my MA in 2012–13. In order to access the scholarship and a place at the university, I had to pay an application fee and attend an interview at UCL. At the time, the application fee was £15, and as I was on unemployment benefits at the time it was hard to find this money and the funds to travel to London for interview. At the time of writing (2017), the application fee at UCL has increased to £75,[30] which is more than the weekly income I had at the point of application. At the interview I was warned that the scholarship was generally awarded to people with exceptional academic backgrounds (which mine was not), and that competition was really tough.

The scholarship I was later awarded, funded by the AHRC, covered fees and maintenance. Even as a scholarship recipient, the funding I accessed during my MA was barely enough to live on, and that was as a single person with no dependants. I had a monthly stipend of about £900 a month, which was less than minimum wage and was expected to cover my living costs in London, where rent was a minimum of £500 a month for the majority of my

---

30 See UCL 'Taught application guidelines' (2017) available at: www.ucl.ac.uk/prospective-students/graduate/taught/application (accessed 25 Sep. 2017).

peers. The AHRC also made stipulations that you couldn't work more than six hours a week to up your income,[31] and I was warned at my interview that the scholarship would not cover my living costs, although I was not given any alternative options. The competitive and low-paid status of the scholarship and application process was demoralising and frustrating, and I am sure many people of a similar status would have given up at that point having failed to obtain funding or due to the restrictive application process.

The funding I accessed has since been taken away from UCL. To my knowledge there is no longer a scholarship in the UK to cover both fees and maintenance costs, which is a massive barrier to any other working-class archivists. Student loans for postgraduate study at MA level were announced recently, but these still only cover tuition fees, and not the accompanying living costs.[32] Without an alternative route into professional roles, workers without socioeconomic privilege cannot progress in their careers. This is not due to lack of skill or passion, but rather to a lack of access to funding the training costs which would enable academic study and qualification.

My journey to qualification was tough, and I lost count of the number of hoops I had to jump through in order to get my study paid for (because I couldn't do so myself). Alongside needing to fund every academic move I've made, I've also been unable to do volunteering and unpaid work (like many of my contemporaries) because I've needed to earn a wage to pay my bills. The assumption that we are all able to find spare time for volunteering to bolster our skill set and acceptability is unfair (especially if this has to be done alongside full-time paid work). This logic fosters the idea that working-class people should be capable and willing to 'go the extra mile' or apply themselves harder than their more affluent peers, in order to achieve goals and reach an equivalent point in their career. This is massively problematic, not to mention impossible, if you have reasons for being unable to work sixty-hour weeks juggling paid and unpaid work, scholarship applications, conferences and professional development, and sleeping! As it now stands, those able to pay their way through academic study access career progression much more easily than those without financial support, and the sector needs to acknowledge that this barrier prohibits it from becoming more diverse and inclusive.

Conclusion

In both of our cases similar issues arose which indicate that funding bodies and archive sector organisations need to re-examine the structures in which they operate and the terms and conditions through which these schemes

---

31 AHRC, 'Studentship grants: terms and conditions and guidance' (2010). See www.ahrc.ac.uk/documents/guides/studentship-grants-terms-conditions-and-guidance/ (accessed 25 Sep. 2017).

32 Government Digital Service, 'Funding for postgraduate study' (2017). See www.gov.uk/postgraduate-loan (accessed 25 Sep. 2017).

are facilitated. When diversity schemes and funding opportunities contain conditions which exclude those the archive profession wants to encourage into its ranks, it cannot expect the workforce to diversify at any speed. To address these problems, these schemes need to be more critically examined, and those whom our profession is keen should take advantage of them need to be consulted.

As qualified professionals in institutions, we also need to re-examine the role that qualification via MA plays in our recruitment and profession. If we want to diversify in our sector then we need to make it possible for people from different backgrounds to enter it. It is not possible to do that and insist upon postgraduate qualification as the minimum entry requirement to professional roles. We need to de-centre academic knowledge as the only valid route to qualification, and reposition it as *one* of the routes to becoming an archivist. This does not devalue the knowledge gained in postgraduate study, but rather creates the necessary space and flexibility to open the profession to other modes of knowledge, particularly that which is gained through learning on the job itself.

Action can be taken through the following steps. The profession can change personal specifications so that the MA is not mandatory (by using a phrase like 'or equivalent professional experience'). We can change funding criteria for scholarships and traineeships to include support for part-time and distance-learning applicants, and ensure maintenance grants are included in all scholarships. We can provide more support after traineeships end, and/ or adapt our traineeships to incorporate funding for study (alongside part-time work, perhaps). We can also use our qualification (if gained) to disperse knowledge and skills to those who need that support, particularly new professionals, para-professional workers, community archivists and those managing collections outside of archive institutions. If those interested in accessing such services don't have the time to do this, their institutions might allow them the space to provide to groups who can. As archive professionals, we have the capacity to make small changes to make our workplaces more accessible and open. These need to be supported and encouraged by sector bodies, universities and managers at higher levels in our organisations.

At the Radical Collections conference, we used our platform to launch the next stage of our research – an online survey titled 'Marginalised in the UK archive sector',[33] through which we have been gathering together qualitative data relating to the experiences of those working in the profession who identify as marginalised. The survey closed for responses in June 2017, and analysis from this data is now in progress. We hope the results will articulate the experiences across workplaces and identity intersections that we often share at conferences, in workplaces and study environments. The data will also be shared with sector bodies managing bursaries, scholarships and

---

33   Hannah Henthorn and Kirsty Fife, 'Marginalised in the UK archive sector' (2017) at https:// goo.gl/forms/7xpPaE7AHaiTkLed2 (accessed 25 Sep. 2017; now closed).

traineeship programmes. We hope our voices can influence the development of future strategy in these areas.

Sara Ahmed writes about job descriptions as brick walls,[34] barriers to progression, professional development and, in many cases for us and many others, barriers to entry into the archive workforce. The act of doing diversity work is 'the feeling of coming up against something that does move'.[35] Key strategic documents by institutions including the ARA and TNA present diversity and inclusion as core to our future direction as archivists and heritage specialists. However, the current structural barriers that exist in our sector workforce mean that many employees from marginalised backgrounds are unable to enter or progress within the profession. In order to achieve these strategic goals we need to examine the brick walls of our own construction, acknowledging our role in their creation, and find ways to rebuild our sector on more inclusive foundations.

34 Ahmed, *Living a Feminist Life*, p. 96.
35 Ibid.

6. Enabling or envisioning politics of possibility? Examining the radical potential of academic libraries

Katherine Quinn

At a time when education as a social right has been reconceived as a private good,[1] ideas of the library collection, library spaces and library work are sites both of troubling marketisation and radical possibility. This chapter will seek to situate the radical educational potential of academic libraries and their publics and to explore different methods through which this potential may be best realised. The library is understood herein as a complex institution with no automatic claims to radical, anti-capitalist or liberatory features. However, the chapter will contest that through a close-level listening to libraries as they already exist, even within this straitened and imperfect context, possibilities for radical educational experiences can be recognised and extended.

With a primary focus on examining the context of higher education (HE) libraries in the UK today, this chapter will explore ways of understanding what I'm calling 'radical possibility'. First, it will situate the library within current debates on the perceived 'crisis' of HE in the UK and contextualise the challenges facing attempts at radical education. In order to set out what fruitful encounters might already be possible it will define a broad and expansive conception of the ideal of radical education as that which allows 'learning without compliance',[2] creativity and engaged self-consciousness. Features of library experiences such as collections, spaces and boundary crossing will be examined in light of their radical potential.

The chapter will then briefly draw on examples to build a case and illustrate the need for radical possibility in libraries. 'Everyday radical librarianship' is introduced here as one approach for enabling radical education and empirical research I carried out in 2014 on library work and self-described 'radical librarianship' is presented. This work situates librarians workers working in HE as the agents of possibility who organise collectively as the loose networking group Radical Librarians Collective (RLC, or 'the collective'). This chapter will

1   J. Holmwood and G.K. Bhambra, 'The attack on education as a social right', *South Atlantic Quarterly* (2012), 111 (2): 392–401. See https://doi.org/10.1215/00382876-1548293 (accessed 4 Jul. 2018).

2   E. Ellsworth, *Places of Learning: Media, Architecture, Pedagogy* (Abingdon: Taylor & Francis, 2004), p. 16.

employ data compiled through interviews and ethnographic observation of an RLC gathering in 2014 (using pseudonyms) to argue that these sorts of worker solidarity, self-education and information dissemination have capacity to strengthen the professional field of critical library and information studies (LIS) while also intervening meaningfully in the lives of university library users.

As a result of the above project, the second case study opens my current PhD research as an alternative approach to envisioning the 'politics of possibility' through library spaces. My ongoing ethnography at the Hive in Worcester, West Midlands, moves from an interpersonal professional focus to the politics of the here and now. The Hive is a joint-use library venture funded through a Private Finance Initiative (PFI) between the University of Worcester and Worcestershire County Council and as such allows multiple viewpoints to converge and challenge assumed norms in both academic and public libraries respectively. My ethnographic methodology considers the library as the space it currently occupies, rather than as the space we might like it to be, so is concerned less with 'enabling' new behaviours and more in 'listening'[3] to the present in ways that illuminate its shortcomings and its already existing radical educational possibility. It seeks to understand how the ostensibly very limiting structures of PFIs, marketised HE and local government interplays with the unknowable encounters, productive conflict and social education between communities of difference. In so doing, the central focus becomes the question asked by J.K. Gibson-Graham: 'how might the potentiality of becoming arise out of the experience of subjection?'.[4]

Situation and challenges of the academic library today

The context for this chapter is one of a reconfigured welfare state in which, starting in the 1970s, education as a social right became reconceived as an individual good.[5] It takes in public and academic libraries and the HE landscape more broadly. Though on the surface similar bodies belonging to different but connected institutions, academic and public libraries illustrate the pulling together and pulling apart of public and higher education more generally. On one level both kinds of libraries are institutions with widely understood and common functions, but they also have complex and divergent ends which have intensified in recent decades as the possibilities of radical social change have been restricted. Public and academic libraries have expanded and contracted almost in sync: the massification of HE in the 1960s[6] took place while public

3   L. Back, The Art of Listening (London: Bloomsbury Academic, 2007).
4   J. Gibson-Graham, The End of Capitalism (as we knew it): a Feminist Critique of Political Economy; with a new introduction (2nd edn.) (Minneapolis, MN: University of Minnesota Press, 2006, p. 23.
5   Holmwood and Bhambra, 'The attack on education as a social right'.
6   Ibid.

libraries were enshrined as a statutory requirement.[7] Though always an uneven and underfunded institution,[8] the orientation towards 'community librarianship' in the 1970s and 1980s enabled public libraries to reach out more effectively to disadvantaged and minority populations.[9] At the same time, the proportion of people in the UK being able to access HE in newly created or converted universities and colleges also expanded. Leap forward to today, and while academic university libraries are growing all the time,[10] their openness is under threat: as HE becomes individually financed and engulfed by quasi-market mechanisms its institutions are restricting access and ideas to anyone who hasn't paid a fee.[11] At the same time, public libraries, once called the 'People's University',[12] are being closed up and down the country.[13]

Many have discussed and debated the 'crisis', or 'crises', of HE[14] in the UK and a full discussion is beyond the scope of this chapter. However, in briefly outlining two important movements in the HE landscape since the second half of the twentieth century I want to draw attention to the way the ecology of the university library is implicated in both. One strand within critical literature on HE in the UK focuses on its marketisation through a reconfigured funding relationship with the state: the decline of central government funding and replacement of individualised student fees, quasi-markets and private providers. The attendant processes of this roll-out of the neoliberal state into the university includes what has been termed the audit explosion.[15] Exercises such as the Research Excellence Framework and continual progress monitoring have been widely criticised as playing 'an important role in neoliberal interventionism in English higher education'[16] and creating an atmosphere of conspicuous production and stress.[17] As well as its mental health implications, this audit environment constitutes

---

7   D. Muddiman, 'Public library outreach and extension 1930–2000', in A. Black and P. Hoare (eds.) *The Cambridge History of Libraries in Britain and Ireland. Volume III: 1850–2000* (Cambridge: Cambridge University Press, 2006), pp. 82–92 at p. 84.

8   A. Black and P. Hoare (eds.) *The Cambridge History of Libraries in Britain and Ireland. Volume III: 1850–2000* (Cambridge: Cambridge University Press, 2006), pp. 82–92, at p. 29.

9   Muddiman, 'Public library outreach and extension', p. 89.

10   SCONUL (2016) 'Evolving spaces and practice', See www.sconul.ac.uk/sites/default/files/documents/Analysis_Evolving_spaces_and_practice_2015.pdf, p. 3 (accessed 30 Jul 2018).

11   M. de Angelis and D. Harvie, '"Cognitive capitalism" and the rat-race: how capital measures immaterial labour in British universities', *Historical Materialism* (2009), 17 (1): 3–30.

12   Black and Hoare (eds.) *Cambridge History of Libraries … Volume III: 1850–2000*, p. 29.

13   A. Wylie, 'Think libraries are obsolete? Think again', www.theguardian.com/public-leaders-network/2016/oct/04/public-libraries-not-obsolete-cuts-closures-protest (accessed 9 Oct. 2017).

14   R. Barnett, *Higher Education: a critical business* (Buckingham: Open University Press, 1997).

15   M. Power, *The Audit Explosion* (London: DEMOS, 1994).

16   J. Cruickshank (2016) 'Putting business at the heart of higher education: on neoliberal interventionism and audit culture in UK universities', *Open Library of Humanities*, 2 (1): 1–33, at 3. See https://doi.org/10.16995/olh.77 (accessed 30 Jul. 2018).

17   R. Gill, 'Breaking the silence: the hidden injuries of neo-liberal academia', in *Secrecy and Silence in the Research Process: feminist reflection* (London: Routledge, 2009).

a loss of academic autonomy for researchers who are increasingly obliged to orientate their outputs towards 'what counts' in current academic trends rather what they deem intellectually important in its own right.[18] Finally, the concurrence of these changes with the individualisation of increasingly high student fees has led to the formation of a service-model of education in which undergraduates are recipients of a product rather than co-producers of public, social, knowledge.[19]

Thinking about this strand of crisis in terms of the academic library, scholarly communications is one area where its influence has been strongly felt. Authors including Harvie et al.,[20] Pirie[21] and Monbiot,[22] have all highlighted the extent to which the marketisation of scholarly communication has created publishing monopolies which not only negatively impact libraries in terms of taking up greater proportions of budgets, but also affect the 'knowledge commons' available to students and researchers. The proportion of library spending going on serials has risen dramatically and unevenly, with problematic differences occurring between the prices of commercial and non-commercial publishing.[23] Beyond budgets, the rise of these commercial publishers and the growing phenomenon of patron-driven acquisition represent at least a partial effect of neoliberalised education in an epistemological as well as practical sense. As currency becomes a proxy for value and usurps other understandings of expertise, collections become increasingly based on marketability. The growing prevalence of resource-list-only physical collections also points to a reimagining of the collection as an idea and a new view of the library itself: the nexus of expertise behind collection development shrinks to that of current faculty and academic trends. While understandable in the current financial climate, the space for serendipity, comprehensiveness and endurance in the library is distorted.

Whereas this first crisis strand can be argued to have affected the academic library from outside, the other crisis highlighted in the critical HE literature refers to a rupture within the academy and concerns 'the loss of faith in the Enlightenment project'.[24] The destabilising epistemology of postmodernism fundamentally challenges the truth claims that many have made, even those defending the idea of the university from markets. In contrast to writers like

18 S. Collini, *What Are Universities For?* (London: Penguin, 2012).

19 J. Winn, 'The co-operative university: labour, property and pedagogy', *Power and Education* (2015), 7 (1): 39–55. See https://doi.org/10.1177/1757743814567386 (accessed 4 Jul. 2018).

20 D. Harvie, G. Lightfoot, S. Lilley and K. Weir, 'What are we to do with feral publishers?', *Organization* (2012), 19 (6): 905–14. See https://doi.org/10.1177/1350508412448859 (accessed 4 Jul. 2018).

21 I. Pirie, 'The political economy of academic publishing', *Historical Materialism* (2009), 17 (3): 31–60. See https://doi.org/10.1163/146544609X12469428108466 (accessed 4 Jul. 2018).

22 G. Monbiot, 'Academic publishers make Murdoch look like a socialist' (2011). See www.theguardian.com/commentisfree/2011/aug/29/academic-publishers-murdoch-socialist (accessed 9 Sep. 2018).

23 Harvie et al., 'What are we to do with feral publishers?', p. 909.

24 Barnett, *Higher Education.*

Collini[25] and Furedi,[26] who tend to base their defence of a publicly funded university system on a memory of its golden years, writers from postcolonial, feminist and class-struggle orientated positions[27] dispute this and demand a more thoroughgoing change. These writers are valuable in not only bemoaning the current state of neoliberalised HE, but also drawing attention to the elitism built into even the public system. They argue that although recent market orientation has done nothing to ameliorate the elitist, and even racist foundations of university research and teachings, neither necessarily did mass education.[28] The second strand of the so-called 'crisis of knowledge' in the academy might be described as a challenge to traditional academic knowledge and the conditions for knowledge creation within the university.

It is within this second crisis strand that radical possibility through library spaces is primarily situated. Two areas are key here: the provision of spaces for spontaneous encounters between diverse knowledges and communities and the role of the library workers in facilitating these opportunities. To begin with spaces, of course there is no automatic claim for libraries to be 'radical' spaces. It has been argued that the growth of public libraries alongside the industrial revolution explicitly ties them to a capitalist disciplining of working class leisure, constituting 'the cheapest police that could possibly be established'.[29] In many ways the intrinsic rush to categorise knowledge is itself restrictive and conservative.[30] However, attention to the spaces made possible in libraries allows us to notice their unique opportunity for education: moments of creation, enchantment, disenchantment and growth are given shape by what knowledge there is, how it is communicated and to what people. The academic library is a space where identities and lives are performed in interaction with the architecture of a community of 'knowledge in the making'.[31] It is a social and performative space, not only in the sense of the people who join in it, but also in the communication between the assembled objects.

25 Collini, *What Are Universities For?.*

26 F. Furedi, *What's Happened to the University? A Sociological Exploration of its Infantalisation* (London: Routledge, 2016).

27 See S. Ahmed, 'Making feminist points' (2013) at: https://feministkilljoys.com/2013/09/11/making-feminist-points/ (accessed 9 Sep. 2017); and A. Emejulu, 'The university is not innocent: speaking of universities', *Verson Books Blog* (29 Mar. 2017) at: www.versobooks.com/blogs/3148-the-university-is-not-innocent-speaking-of-universities (accessed 4 Jul. 2018).

28 Emejulu, 'The university is not innocent'; and J. Holmwood, 'The idea of the university', in Holmwood (ed.) *A Manifesto for the Public University* (London: Bloomsbury, 2011), p. 19.

29 Joseph Brotherton quoted in E. Hayes and A. Morris, 'Leisure role of public libraries', *Journal of Librarianship and Information Science* (2005), 37 (3): 75–81, at 77. See https://doi.org/10.1177/0961000605057480 (accessed 4 Jul. 2018).

30 See A. Billey, E. Drabinski and K.R. Roberto, 'What's gender got to do with it? A critique of RDA 9.7', *Cataloging and Classification Quarterly* (2014), 52 (4): 412–21 at: https://doi.org/10.1080/01639374.2014.882465 (accessed 4 Jul. 2018).

31 C. Camic, N. Gross and M. Lamont (eds.) *Social Knowledge in the Making* (Chicago, IL: University of Chicago Press, 2011).

The library's uniqueness here lies in part in its paradoxically historical and ever-changing complexion. In a sense, a library is a static, historical, conservative entity – a 'walled-garden'. As Drabinski has recently argued, collections can only ever present 'one possible world',[32] and they're always on the back foot. Yet at the same time, libraries are dynamic, always evolving, always being updated. Even with slow-moving collections, the connections that can be made across shelves, and between shelves and their ever-changing patrons, is in constant negotiation. Its users bring formal and tacit knowledge to a library, and the connections they make between objects and people have the capacity to be emotional as well as intellectual. Foucault's famous quotation about the fantasia of the library speaks to the elusive power of collected knowledges: 'the imaginary is not formed in opposition to reality as its denial or compensation; it grows among signs, from book to book, in the interstice of repetitions and commentaries; it is born and takes shape in the interval between books'.[33] As such, I am interested in the possibility that emerges from attending to this notion of the 'imaginary' in the material conditions of the library. In what ways can non-compliant, unbounded and enchanting educational experiences be better fostered by library spaces and work focused on the idea of radical possibility?

Before describing the two empirical strategies I have used to explore radical possibility in library spaces, I will explain my choice of the concept 'radical'. As a term that is paradoxically ubiquitous both within politically left and right vocabularies, the word often eludes definition or is defined in problematic and even contradictory terms. In many ways using it at all seems pointless. In choosing to do so I keep in mind the Marxist sociologist Stuart Hall's sentiment in relation to the similarly slippery term of 'neoliberal'. Hall defended his loyalty to the term – 'however unsatisfactory' – since to him it represented a 'first approximation' that can have 'further determinations' added to it during the course of analysis. In continuing to use it, he acknowledged the 'political necessity' of having focus and a 'cutting edge'.[34] With 'radical', I acknowledge its reductive capacity, but think it sets an emphasis on anti-capitalist, non-compliant, and autonomous thought and action that 'activist', 'progressive' or 'democratic' do not quite attain.

Though clearly in conversation with its opposites, radical should not only be considered as a reaction, and thus is also considered here in reference to an

32 E. Drabinski, 'Are libraries neutral?'. See www.emilydrabinski.com/are-libraries-neutral/ (accessed 13 Feb. 2018), n.p.

33 M. Foucault, D. Bouchard and S. Simon (trans.), 'The fantasia of the library', in Michel Foucault: Language Counter-Memory, Practice. Selected essays and interviews' (Ithaca, NY: Cornell University Press, 1996),

34 Stuart Hall, 'The neo-liberal revolution', Cultural Studies (2011), 25 (6): 705–28 at 706. See https://doi.org/10.1080/09502386.2011.619886 (accessed 4 Jul. 2018).

unknown,[35] risk-laden,[36] creative and potentially wonderful[37] possibility. While anger and rejection of the dehumanising capacity of disciplining neoliberal education is legitimate, radical also alludes to a creative unknown which presents an opportunity in the space of the library, however tentative. Radical education can hereby be associated with an active process of becoming, the possibility of learning experiences that enhance both individual self-consciousness and dignity under capitalism.[38] It is also contributing to social engagement and shared communities. This agrees with hooks' view of the possibility of education as 'enabling' and as 'enhancing our capacity to be free'[39] – suggesting its outcome – while also seeing the process of learning itself as an opportunity for 'noncompliance and knowledge in the making', as Ellsworth argues.[40]

Thinking about libraries rather than class or seminar rooms, the space for radical possibility can come about in several ways. Libraries are uniquely positioned as spaces for undirected learning, where choices can be made and tangents can be followed without necessarily being restricted by time or remit. Librarians have a role in creating an environment without restrictions, and facilitating the individual goals of the library's diverse groups. The next section highlights the two cases through which I've sought to better understand this radical possibility.

'Enabling' radical education?

My first approach to the question of radical possibility in university libraries was contingent on the idea that such educational experiences could be 'enabled' by library workers and education in LIS departments. As such, the data collected were aimed at understanding the perceptions and experiences of self-described 'radical librarians' as they attempted to work and organise within HE institutions according to their political convictions. I became involved in RLC first as an individual and then as a researcher, and obtained consent from those organising the 2014 national gathering in London.

The collective came about in 2013 through an accumulation of serendipitous exchanges between like-minded library workers on the social media site Twitter. These initial conversations were sparked by expressions of frustration 'about increasing commodification and marketisation in libraries, about creeping neoliberalism and managerialist attitudes within the profession, about the decimation of the public library system, and much

---

35 Ellsworth, *Places of Learning*, p. 6.
36 b. hooks, *Teaching to Transgress* (London: Routledge, 1994), p. 4.
37 S. Ahmed, *The Cultural Politics of Emotion* (2nd edn.) (Edinburgh: Edinburgh University Press, 2014), p. 178.
38 P. Freire, *Education for Critical Consciousness* (London: Bloomsbury, 2013).
39 hooks, *Teaching to Transgress*, p. 4.
40 Ellsworth, *Places of Learning*, p. 17.

more'.[41] The initial formation of RLC was described by interviewee James as a cathartic moment of 'Do you think what I think? I think I think what you think … we should do something about this!'. Interviewee Jane described the realisation that these encounters meant they 'were not alone'[42]. These exclamations are an expression of the feeling of release shared among people who otherwise did not know each other, and of their happiness at being relieved of what felt like isolation in their respective workplaces. They also speak to the isolation associated with work in capitalism.

Since then, the collective has focused on maintaining an online presence for conversation, collaboration and research. It has a Twitter feed, website, an open access journal and a series of online collaborative documents aimed at information sharing and solidarity. While the readership is not prescribed and no formal membership exists, the resources include reading lists, guides and strategies primarily useful to fellow library workers. Offline, physical meetups have taken place at five annual gatherings across the UK in Bradford, London, Huddersfield, Brighton and Glasgow. There have also been sporadic regional meetings in London, Oxford, Yorkshire and Dublin in between the big gatherings.

Political positions from the collective are deliberately not clearly defined. Keeping the term 'radical' as undefined beyond its etymological definition of 'grasping at the root' of librarianship was a tactic designed to promote inclusivity. Although such claims to universality could be problematic, this root appeared a lot to do with democratic values of free information, and a belief that such information could enable politically engaged non-compliant education. Alice described her personal political position and occupational identity as a librarian in the same breath, saying 'I always came from a relatively active political position anyway … and became a librarian because I found libraries really scary when I was a student and I realised that there had to be a way where it wasn't scary, because information should be empowering and you should be able to help people find information'.[43] Jane talked about how the 'institutional baggage' of university settings stifles personal commitments to librarianship. As such, these members felt that an important aspect of the collective's role was to facilitate conversations and meetings between people who identified themselves by their work, perceived the existence of librarianship's 'radical root', but saw their paid-work detracting from it.

As a collective, RLC aims to organise inclusive politics 'prefiguratively', to use James' description.' They defined this as: 'doing things as you want them to be', aligning with a common anarchist notion of prefiguration, which is the 'embodiment, within the ongoing political practice of a movement, of those

41 B. Brynolf, 'A history of the radical librarians collective' at https://rlc.radicallibrarianship.org/about-2/history-of-rlc/ (accessed 9 Sep. 2017).

42 Quinn and Bates, 'Resisting neoliberalism'.

43 K. Quinn, *Resisting Neoliberalism: the Challenge of Activist Librarianship Within the UK HE Context* (Sheffield: University of Sheffield, 2014). See http://dagda.shef.ac.uk/dispub/dissertations/2013-14/External/Quinn_130117685.pdf (accessed 9 Sep. 2017).

forms of social relations, decision-making, culture and human experience that are the ultimate goal'.[44] This value is carried into the collective's organisational structure through aiming to remove (formal) hierarchies, using spaces for gatherings that share anti-capitalist values for the annual gatherings (such as the London Action Resource Centre, the Cowley Club social centre co-op and the Women's Library Glasgow), and using tools like reflection to critically assess their actions within institutions which they feel constrain them. Among RLC's core interests are the promotion of critical information skills, web privacy, defence of public libraries through supporting local and national campaigns and union organisation against declining working conditions across sectors. Such values highlight their political as opposed to purely professional identity concerns, and a desire to connect librarianship with broader societal concerns. Thus, the collective operates as an alternative to the official professional body for librarians – the Chartered Institute for Library and Information Professionals (CILIP) – which one of my interviewees called 'utterly pointless', and which has been criticised for aiming at unattainable political neutrality.

Everyday practices were a particularly interesting element of the interviews which covered radical librarianship. So-called 'guerrilla collection development'[45] involves using what institutional leverage was available to interviewees – in this case their budget – to 'secretly develop a whole alternative collection' of challenging texts for library users to benefit from. In particular it demonstrates a desire to disrupt the dominance of marketability as a proxy for value, and mitigate actively against silenced voices in the library collection, a point brought up by two interviewees. They felt this was entirely within their remit as subject librarians, since the 'alternative voices' are valid, but may be overlooked: 'it's about combatting where the dominance is really I think … and encouraging people to believe that those are OK sources to be using as well, and critiquing the state of play'.[46] Recently Hudson has argued insightfully against believing 'diversity' is sufficient for anti-racist library development, saying 'to be included in a space is not necessarily to have agency within that space'.[47] However it seems an important, if small-scale, act of resistance.

Further practices of radical librarians were articulated as daily interactions with students or the public in the workplace. These included talking to students about their assignments in an honest and emotionally invested way, suggesting challenging topics and material and even talking about the proprietary nature of many of the technologies their workplace institution rely on. One interviewee suggested that librarians in general were too concerned about 'balance' and overestimated the 'danger' of having divergent opinions.

44　C. Boggs, quoted in Winn, 'The co-operative university', p. 45.

45　Quinn and Bates, 'Resisting neoliberalism', p. 328.

46　Quinn, Resisting Neoliberalism.

47　D.J. Hudson, 'On "diversity" as anti-racism in library and information studies: a critique', Journal of Critical Library and Information Studies (2017), 1: 1–36 at 13.

There was a tension here between ethics and legality, especially around questions of copyright. As one interviewee queried: 'how much "ethically" as a librarian are you allowed to scrabble around trying to find a free, probably illegal copy of a document that you find on the internet? And how much shouldn't you do that? And ... I think ... we're not allowed to have those kinds of conversations within the library service'.[48] Having these conversations, even if stopping short of providing the 'illegal' PDF, is important for enriching understanding of the political economy of academic publishing, but poses a personal risk to librarians employed by university institutions.

Although the collective has many strong points, both in terms of offering mutual aid to self-identifying radical librarians and in terms of intervening in students' everyday lives, I found that some areas within it need improving. First, although its horizontal and open nature is often alluded to, without deliberate processes or structures it was hard to know what or who RLC really was, and this gave rise to informal hierarchies which were difficult to navigate.[49] Balancing the desire to focus on issues pertinent to those attending a gathering with a stated desire to be radical must also be constantly re-evaluated. If issues are self-selected, there's a tendency for status quo concerns to be tacitly supported, even within these radical groups. As Ahmed argues, 'open' calls with 'invisible' restrictions (who is speaking, who is attending, what is being discussed), work to reproduce rather than resist 'what we inherit' in terms of class, ethnicity, gender and ability.[50] As she says, 'it would be timely to re-state the arguments that sexism and racism are not incidental but structural, and thus to understand sexism and racism, requires better, closer readings of what is being gathered. Attending to the restrictions in the apparently open spaces of a social world brings us into closer proximity to an actual world'. This is a question for the entire LIS field, not just RLC, but for a collective with the above-stated aims it would seem highly appropriate to focus on such issues.

As I have elaborated elsewhere,[51] RLC has addressed many of these criticisms, with such positive developments as more explicit processes and named organising committees having been put in place.[52] Being critical and reflective practitioners necessitates a willingness to visit and revisit aims, structures and practices, and also to learn from where others have gone before. To this end, a constructive collaborative document entitled 'Barriers for change' was created in 2016,[53] and resources from other anticapitalist

48 Quinn, *Resisting Neoliberalism*.
49 Quinn and Bates, 'Resisting neoliberalism'.
50 Ahmed, *The Cultural Politics of Emotion*.
51 Quinn and Bates, 'Resisting neoliberalism'.
52 See the 'Who is RLC?' page on the Radical Librarians Collective website at https://rlc.radicallibrarianship.org/who-is-rlc/ (accessed 9 Sep. 2017).
53 This document was quickly updated and renamed 'Follow-up to "barriers to engagement"'. See https://rlc.radicallibrarianship.org/2017/03/08/follow-up-to-barriers-to-engagement/ (accessed 9 Sep. 2017).

organising groups were flagged up for possible training. Overall, the collective has the potential to become a space through which radical alternatives to neoliberal hegemony within librarianship can be explored and fostered.

Attending to the library as a living space

My new research – and my second example – is more concerned with the life of the library as it is and attempts to move away from a 'capitalocentric' reading of the space, and of librarians as the primary agents for encouraging radical possibility. 'Capitalocentric' refers to a framing of reality whereby all 'non-capitalist' alternatives are connected and contingent on a dominant and dominating conception of capitalist society.[54] 'Alternatives' such as RLC therefore become 'capitalism's other'[55] and 'cannot help but disappoint' next to its strength. Such a reading creates a bifurcated society, which denies its messiness and openness and places unrealisable expectations on 'activism'. Instead, asking Gibson-Graham's question, 'how might the potentiality of becoming arise out of the experience of subjection?'[56] places emphasis on an envisioning of the present that identifies and draws out moments of rupture. These moments may not 'remake our societies overnight in some total and millennial fashion' but could move us towards everyday reconstitution.[57]

This time, I am centrally interested in the capacity of ethnography as a methodology to illuminate notions of educational becoming, difference and convergence within daily experiences in a library. Radical possibility is sought in the spaces between the shelves and illuminates more subtle (or even more mundane) expressions of non-compliant education than the formal project of radical librarianship. The example I have chosen is the Hive, a joint-use public-academic library in Worcester. As such, with its integrated public and academic collections, the library's capacity for intellectual and emotional 'boundary crossing' is elevated, as is the possibility of destabilising problematic academic truth claims as they are negotiated between a more diverse community. However, my preliminary research indicates that these substantial radical possibilities also come with a heightened capacity for the projection and internalisation of subtle classification and hierarchy. For example, the treatment and self-identification of university students vis à vis their public neighbours can give way to collaboration and empathy on the one hand, or judgement and the hardening of boundaries on the other. I am using concepts such as empathy, worth and affect to better understand these processes.

My close-level ethnography relies on an epistemic belief in the politicised nature of research, making the approach itself part and parcel of a construction

---

54   Gibson-Graham, *The End of Capitalism*, p. 125.

55   Ibid., p. 7.

56   Ibid., p. 23.

57   Ibid., p. 254.

of knowledge that is 'challenging and transforming … of the uses and abuses of power'.[58] In practice, I have been following the ethnographic methods of close reflective journal-keeping and have supplemented this written and doodled data with interviews of library workers at the Hive, as well as less-structured ethnographic interviews with library patrons. As Taussig argues,[59] whereas taking a photo 'freezes time', drawing an image creates 'a reality, encompassing time' and I have been using this close-level attention to allow moments of empathy, emotional charge and atmospheric shifts to become part of how I think about the life of the library. In contrast to the RLC research, this time I have been able to attend to and dwell on the activity in it over a sustained period – one academic year. My own affective reaction to the space and interaction with it has been written and drawn into my analysis, making my observations perhaps more subtle, but also more attentive than a short, intensive set of interviews with staff only.

Taking these theoretical and methodological concerns together, I also explore the extent to which the structure and culture of the Hive internalises or subverts the neoliberalising trends of academic libraries:

- What does the life of joint-use libraries contribute to our understanding of the state and status of HE libraries in the UK today? (considering collections, teaching and built space)
- How are conceptions of knowledge, community and critical education negotiated in a joint-use library, and how far could these libraries represent a rupture in the privatisation of academic knowledge and communities? Is the Hive a fruitful alternative to the privatisation of knowledge and space in HE?
- How does engagement with lived encounters between people and objects in a joint-use library illuminate our understanding of the agencies of public and academic libraries, and strengthen possibilities for radical social education?
- In what ways has the institutionalisation of libraries through public management, professionalisation and corporatisation of HE affected the self-conceptions of librarians' agency to promote critical education?

In attending to these questions my research does not aim to be a case-study or to argue for scientifically defined pros and cons of joint-use libraries. Ethnographic work necessarily produces situated knowledge, and the end result will be a situated work which celebrates the peculiarities of the Hive while using its insights to think more broadly about the radical possibility of libraries, and about reimagining their futures. While this research into RLC allowed a way into library workers' perceptions of their challenges and

---

58 R. Nandagiri, 'Why feminism: some notes from "the field" on doing feminist research' (2017). See http://blogs.lse.ac.uk/gender/2017/10/12/why-feminism-some-notes-from-the-field-on-doing-feminist-research/ (accessed 10 Oct. 2017).

59 M. Taussig, *I Swear I Saw This: Drawings in Fieldwork Diaries, Namely My Own* (Chicago, IL and London: University of Chicago Press, 2011).

possibilities on the library floor, it works from the ground level up and allows subtle moments of radical education to be exposed and extended.

This chapter has outlined themes coalescing with a call to listen more closely to the radical possibilities of academic libraries, situating the library within the transformed and transforming landscape of HE in the UK and the wider state. It has argued that the state of HE vis-à-vis neoliberalisation and other underlying epistemic assumptions shapes and colours the library and the work it does. The chapter has explored one perspective through a worker-level study on the RLC on the theme of encouraging radical education. In concluding, it has switched focus to the ground level and explored how close-level ethnography may allow a more expansive and enriching reading of radical possibility. In doing so, the chapter has aimed to illuminate the life of the library itself for those who use it, allowing them to better understand its radical and hopeful potential.

Index

CPSIA information can be obtained
at www.ICGtesting.com
Printed in the USA
BVHW021634221218
536193BV00023B/186/P